THE DOOR TO WITCHCRAFT

the door to
WITCHCRAFT

A New Witch's Guide
TO HISTORY, TRADITIONS & MODERN-DAY SPELLS

TONYA A. BROWN

ILLUSTRATIONS BY CHLOÉ BESSON

ALTHEA
PRESS

Interior and Cover Designer: Emma Hall
Art Producer: Sue Bischofberger
Editor: Pippa White
Production Editor: Erum Khan
Illustrations © 2019 Chloé Besson

ISBN: Print 978-1-64152-399-8 | eBook 978-1-64152-400-1

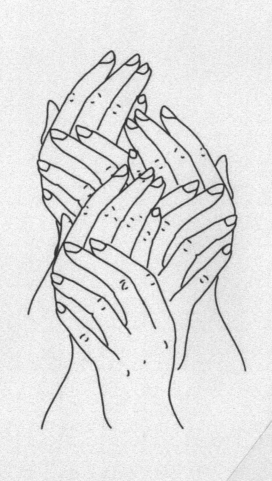

This book is dedicated to the three strong, amazing women who raised me:

Erin Brown,

Kandi Meadors,

and Jill Fields.

CONTENTS

Introduction   viii

PART I: WITCHCRAFT AND PRACTICAL MAGIC   1
1 Understanding Witchcraft   2
2 Core Beliefs and Values   23
3 How to Tap into Your Powers   35
4 How to Practice Witchcraft   56

PART II: SPELLS   87
5 Love   90
6 Health and Healing (in Yourself and Others)   108
7 Career   122
8 Friends and Family Matters   136
9 Spiritual Work   150
10 Protection   164

Glossary   179
Resources   182
References   184
Index   187

INTRODUCTION

If you have picked up this book, there is a good chance that the world of witchcraft has enticed you. Whether it incites a light curiosity or a passionate craving, witchcraft is a personal pursuit that you can adapt to fit your goals. Do you want to be an herbal witch with a warm home filled with dried herbs and tinctures? Do you seek to connect to the spirit world for meaningful messages? Does the idea of glamour magic fill you with seductive power? Or do you simply want to hone your skills of intuition? What a lot of people don't realize is that witchcraft does not have just one purpose or one school of thought. Instead, it is a labyrinth of opportunities and a way to fine-tune your unique blend of magic. As the editor in chief of *Witch Way Magazine*, my goal has always been to empower readers to find what sparks their passion. Magic isn't about doing a spell in a particular way; it's about practicing in whatever way works for you. The goal of this book is to help you discover what your way is and how wonderful witchcraft can be.

As a child, I always felt different. I had quite a few spiritual encounters. I didn't know it then, but it was witchcraft calling out to me. I was too young to fully comprehend that the universe was telling me something: I was a witch. I grew up in a Christian community, and everything I read about witchcraft tied it to the Wiccan religion. I thought my choice of identity was limited to either being a Christian or a Wiccan, and honestly, neither felt right to me. Over the years,

I've come to learn that Wicca and witchcraft aren't the same thing, and that being interested in the world of magic doesn't need to have an impact on your religious faith (or lack thereof) if you don't want it to. My skills and abilities did not feel tied to a religious belief because they weren't.

Witchcraft offers the ability to be a part of a community, as well as the chance to be true to yourself. Since I began my journey, I have discovered plenty of places within the magical realm where I feel that I fit. I can't wait to share them with you and help you discover your own!

Witchcraft is about creating your own place within spirituality. Do you enjoy rituals? Does your soul sing when you see the moon? Do you have a tarot deck itching to be played with? Do you enjoy creating oils? These things are common among witches, but your answers to these questions do not dictate your authenticity as a witch. If you are someone who feels drawn to mysticism in any way, if you seek to discover life's mysteries, or if the label "witch" feels comfortable or intriguing to you—then you, my amazing reader, are a witch. And I wrote this book for you.

WITCHCRAFT AND PRACTICAL MAGIC

The best way to figure out which parts of witch-craft are going to appeal to you is by learning enough to create a foundation for yourself. To be a witch of substance, you've got to know a little history, what the core beliefs and values of witch-craft are, how to access your powers, and the various ways to practice your craft. Those are the topics we will explore in part I.

CHAPTER I

UNDERSTANDING WITCHCRAFT

Let's start with the basics. In this chapter, we'll define key terminology, discuss who is and is not a witch, and briefly learn history that every witch must know.

WHAT IS WITCHCRAFT?

A witch, by modern definition, is anyone who practices witchcraft. Witchcraft is not a religion. It is a craft—something that we do with our hands, our minds, and our energy.

I think my very first introduction to the idea of witchcraft was in the beloved cult classic *Hocus Pocus*. The movie is about the Sanderson sisters—evil, hag-type women who declare that they must take the lives of children to stay young and beautiful forever. This depiction is the classic interpretation of witches: ugly, child-killing, and full of bad intentions. While this image understandably comes from many years of religious and cultural fear, it's not the truth by any means.

Witchcraft is an empowering practice that any person can learn, cultivate, and personalize. It is all about stepping outside of our mundane world and choosing to take on a perspective of mysticism and reverence for nature, life, and the energetic forces of this world. But what makes witch-craft simply intoxicating is that it's about appreciating the world around us. It's not just about what we *can* see; it's about everything in between. It is the love for spirits, messages, otherworldliness, unexplainable things, mysterious connec-tions, and the universal system of checks and balances. That is witchcraft.

Witchcraft is about taking the raw, beautiful, and pow-erful forces of our world and using them to create change. While the media isn't completely wrong in their representa-tions of witches—I love my divination cards just as much as Wendy Beauchamp from *Witches of East End*—witches are *not* all leaning over our cauldrons as green slime boils for a life-sucking ritual. Sanderson sisters, I'm looking at you! Witchcraft is about finding the way that you personally can best manipulate energy. Witchcraft (and this book) is about helping you nurture those skills.

ARE YOU A WITCH?

"Being a Witch is about having your eyes wide open and experiencing the whole onslaught of existence."
—FIONA HORNE, *Witch: A Magickal Journey*

In recent years, the word *witch* has taken on quite a power-ful meaning. Not only does it define someone who practices witchcraft, but it's also come to symbolize those in our culture who are willing to stand strong for their beliefs—especially when it comes to human rights. Many people of all races, ages, and genders are standing up in the face of adversity and stating that they are witches.

So, are you a witch? Well, the fact that you're interested in the subject means that you may already identify as one. If the label "witch" feels good and makes you feel powerful, or if you seek to create change in your life using magical practices, then, yes, you may be a witch. There are so many misconceptions about what it means to be a witch, so let's start by breaking some of those down before we explore the traits that witches tend to have in common.

Paganism vs. Wicca vs. Witchcraft

Although these three things are connected, they do not always go hand in hand. Let's discuss the differences.

∴ **Paganism simply states what you are not.** A pagan is defined as "a person holding religious beliefs other than those of the main world religions" according to the Oxford English Dictionary. So, a pagan is anyone who doesn't follow the teachings of Christianity, Islam, Hinduism, Buddhism, Sikhism, and Judaism. Anyone else, witch or not, is a pagan.

∴ **Wicca is a religion.** It is a religion based around pre-Christian traditions with hierarchies, rules, and a form of governance.

∴ **Witchcraft is about what you do.** Someone who practices witchcraft is a person who attempts to change and manipulate energy to their will.

You can be all three of these things, none, or a unique combination that you choose. So, for example, a Christian witch is not Wiccan or pagan. Quite a few witches are non-theistic. Plus, there are Wiccans who worship without choosing to practice witchcraft.

However you identify, figuring out how you best relate to these three words will save you a lot of time when choosing events, books, and other ways to curate your practice.

Misconceptions

As mentioned, the most common fallacy I hear is that you must be Wiccan to be a witch. This couldn't be further from the truth. You do not have to dedicate yourself to any religion to be a witch. If you are comitted to learning how to manipulate energy—whether it be with **herbals**, spirits, rituals, or spell work, feel free to call yourself a witch!

Another misconception is that all witches are women, and that men are something different like warlocks, wizards, or magicians. Language is a living medium and it constantly changes. If a person of any gender wants to call themself a witch—or a wizard, warlock, or magician—and this word fuels their power and gives them the confidence to do their craft, then they should own it! No one has the right to judge the validity of how someone chooses to label themselves.

I also often hear that to be a proper witch, you must memorize old Latin verses, which just isn't true. Committing blessings to memory does have a place in some witchcraft traditions, but this is not a requirement. If you find that practiced rhymes lull you into a meditative trance and help you connect to the universe or spirit world, rock on! If you find that closing your eyes and speaking in the moment and from the gut is best, then that is just as witchy as anything else.

Lastly, a misconception I often hear is that in order to be a witch, you must be a part of a coven. Covens are real, and they are something many witches crave since they are communities (and can truly be like families). However, magic is personal, and finding people who practice exactly as you do is rare. If you have the opportunity to find such a community, I encourage you to join it, but don't hesitate to practice alone as you see fit. It does not make you any less of a witch.

I am a big believer in owning your power. Once you find what works for you, don't let anyone tell you it's not good enough. Follow your instincts.

Witchy Inclinations

What are the signs that you may already be a witch? (I promise this is much less scary than looking up symptoms on WebMD!) Let's go over some things that many witches find they have in common.

You were considered a "weird kid." Many witches share that when they were younger, they didn't quite fit in with the crowd. While it's true that everyone feels like they are an outsider at some point in their lives, witches tend to see the world in a way that others do not. The best way to describe it is to say that they typically see the world from the outside in. In kids and teens, this usually manifests as an interest in media that expresses an atypical point of view. For instance, you may have found yourself indulging in non-mainstream music, film, or other media. Or perhaps your opinions didn't match those of your peers and were considered "odd."

Nature speaks to you intimately. A lot of witches find that they deeply connect with nature. Many fondly remember a time when they stared up at the moon and *felt it* for the first time, or palpably sensed the energy from a tree, or experienced the intimacy of digging their feet in the dirt. Nature is a big part of what grounds us as humans, and many witches feel nature's pull acutely. Many say that being in nature is the thing that makes them feel the calmest. Witches also frequently report that animals have always trusted them more than other humans.

Witchcraft and Womanhood

Witchcraft has been connected to women since it was conve- nient to persecute them for it. While men have practiced magic for just as long, it is women who have paid the toll for its power. Over 75 percent of the victims of witch hunts throughout his- tory have been female. After centuries of death, it is that strong, screaming, overpowering feminine energy that has woven itself into the foundation of our witchcraft practices. For this reason, the female is often regarded higher than her male counterparts in many witchcraft traditions.

The female is said to be ruled by the moon, with its phases having a direct impact on her emotional self and physical body— namely through her menstrual cycle. Women are also creators of life. (This is why there was so much emphasis on the womb in pre-Christian worship. Statues of large, voluptuous women were created by many ancient cultures, as the female body is the ulti- mate symbol of fertility.)

As beautiful and inspiring as it is to think of fertility as the source of magic, we can't get too caught up in that idea. Our magic and our identity as witches do not stem from our genitals—all are able to tap into this type of energy equally.

With that in mind, feminine energy is often called "lunar energy" because of the female connection to the moon. This energy is defined as nurturing, emotional, caring, giving, and comfort- ing. Conversely, masculine energy is known as "solar energy" and is based off the sun. This type of energy is fiery, passionate, forward-moving, ambitious, and action-oriented. I've seen some authors say that women who possess solar qualities are lesser than or need to be fixed, and that men are undeserving to work within the lunar. We've grown too much as a society to encourage such bias and hate-mongering.

Whether you are a badass woman who oozes solar energy or a gorgeous man who drips lunar, or a nonbinary person with an energy all your own, you are a powerful, strong witch.

You blame the moon. Scientists have proven that the moon has an effect on our energies, bodies, and minds on a daily basis. As with nature, though, witches seem to feel the moon's pull more than others. When you are feeling "off" or notice that your colleagues are behaving differently from usual, have you found yourself Googling what phase the moon is in? Or do you ever look up at the moon at night and know that you won't get a good night's sleep based on its current phase?

You feel power surges from the environment. When energy overwhelms your physical space, you feel the power course through you. Lightning storms are a perfect example. You may feel energy gathering in your hands, chest, or gut during these moments.

You're sensitive to people's energy. Energy plays a large role in witchcraft. You may find that being in a crowded grocery store or a club can feel overwhelming because of all the different energies flying around. Beyond group energy, you may be especially receptive to the feelings and concerns of individuals. Naturally this can be overwhelming, so witches have developed a variety of methods for protecting ourselves from being derailed by rogue energy. We will cover this later in the book.

You might like the macabre. Due to the outside-in perspective, many witches see death as a natural transition. You may find interest in things most consider "spooky" such as skulls, snakes and snakeskins, spirits, and other curious oddities.

You embrace your psychic ability when you find it. A lot of witches have a natural ability to tap into the spirit world. Due to our heightened sense of being able to feel energies, we are more likely to embrace any psychic abilities we possess. A common manifestation of this is seeing, feeling, or experiencing the presence of ghosts. Most witches seem to find this more interesting than scary, though everyone has their own personal experience, of course. I believe that everyone has some type of psychic ability, but witches who are aware of energy notice theirs sooner and nurture it.

Terminology and Types of Witches

While many of us wish we could live in a world with no labels, they can also be a powerful way to claim ownership and identity. Finding a word for who you are or how you feel can be quite empowering. That said, don't get too hung up on the labels below, especially since I only mention a handful of them. You can be rocking the kitchen witchery by day and be a seductive glam witch by night. Your magic is as beautiful and unique as you are.

GREEN WITCH A green witch works primarily with nature and herbals. This category encompasses kitchen witches, hearth witches, garden witches, and herbal witches. These practices focus on using the power of plants and food to harness energy and create change.

GLAM WITCH A glam witch uses their abilities to draw attention either toward or away from themself. This is ideal for seduction magic as well as blending in when it's needed. Glam witches use all the tools in their arsenal such as colors, scents, and aesthetics to manipulate how they are perceived.

FOLK WITCHES A folk witch uses traditions that have been passed down through generations. This term can include family traditions, rootwork, voodoo, hoodoo, *stregheria*, *brujería*, and other witchcraft practices. These practices are typically focused on practical witchery, creating change in one's life, and working with the spirits or ancestors around us.

TRADITIONAL WITCHES A traditional witch follows structured paths such as Alexandrian Wicca or Gardnerian Wicca. These paths are considered religions, and they follow specific guidelines that are based on a lineage (meaning that traditions are handed down through generations of Wiccan priestesses— like a magical family tree). This type of path is ideal for those who like ceremonial magic and prefer to be guided with structure and rules.

ECLECTIC WITCHES An eclectic witch takes what works for them and leaves what doesn't. They may love a ritual from a traditional religion while leaving behind other guidelines they don't like. This is ideal for witches who find power in exploring everything.

NECROMANCERS A necromancer works with the dead and spirits. You'll find that witches from this group communicate with the dead and are skilled in divination practices. Their spell work typically revolves around assistance from the spirits.

What's in a Name: Warlocks

Warlock is an Old English term meaning someone who is a traitor or a liar. For this reason, many witches cringe at the word. It's generally not considered good etiquette to call someone a warlock. That said, the word has recently started to become synonymous with *sorcerer*. So if someone feels at home using that label, follow their lead, since labels change when people own them in new ways.

THE HISTORY OF WITCHCRAFT

"Witches aren't monsters; they're just women . . .
they're fucking women who cum and giggle and
play in the night and that's why everyone wants to
set them on fire, because they're fucking jealous."
—ILANA GLAZER, *Broad City*

While it might seem boring to go over the history of witchcraft,
remember that knowledge is power. I guarantee that one day
someone will come to you with a bunch of factually incorrect
information about witchcraft. If you can spot the falsehoods,
you'll know who to listen to and who to invest time in.

Throughout recorded history, witchcraft has been revered,
but also persecuted. To fully appreciate our ability to practice
witchcraft openly today, we must look back to see where we've
been. The Salem witch trials are infamous, but sadly there
have been much deadlier witch hunts.

The following timeline is in no way complete, but here
are some important moments you need to know.

The divide between men and women is created.
Tertullian, a Christian philosopher, states in *De Cultu Feminarum* that women are inherently lesser than men and that they are the devil's gateway to our world.

197 CE

The first woman is formally executed for heresy; the witch stereotype is set.
The king of France, King Robert, approves the trial of over a dozen individuals for practicing religious heresy, including one woman. During this trial, she is accused of orgies, worshipping demonic entities, and killing children, ultimately defining the witch stereotype.

1022 CE

The first documented witch hunt occurs.
Alice Kyteler, a wealthy Irish woman, is charged with witchcraft after outliving several husbands. She is accused of practicing the dark arts, having intercourse with demons, and using "lotions and spells" with friends to conjure up evil spirits. This trial leads to at least 11 others close to Kyteler accused and put on trial, with some executed.

1324 CE

900 CE

Women are considered consorts of the devil.
A document (*canon Episcopi*) is recorded by Regino of Prüm, a German monk, stating that women can be perverted by the devil, and ride into the night with the goddess Diana.

1231 CE

Death for "failure of faith" is ordered by the church.
Pope Gregory IX decrees execution as the punishment for anyone who refuses to adhere to the *correct* faith (Christianity), instituting the Papal Inquisition.

As many as 500,000 people are executed as witches across Europe. After the first witch hunt and the popularization of the *Malleus Maleficarum*, the witch craze gains momentum in Europe. Of the people executed, 85 percent are women.

1400–1700 CE

England lifts its witchcraft law. England lifts the law that imprisoned accused witches. This is the end of the European witch craze, and the event that encourages Gerald Gardner to step out into the spotlight, publicly declare himself as a witch, and share the religion of Wicca with the world, giving birth to many modern Wicca and witchcraft movements.

1951 CE

1486 CE

The *Malleus Maleficarum* is first published. This book by Heinrich Kramer (translated as *The Hammer of Witches*) becomes the most popular guide to finding and torturing witches. It becomes the basis for many superstitions about witches.

1692–1693 CE

Over 200 people are accused in the Salem witch trials. Mass hysteria overwhelms the town of Salem, Massachusetts, as more than 200 women and men are accused of witchcraft, with 19 ultimately executed.

Paganism and the Seeds of Witchcraft

> "*Pagan* comes from the Latin *paganus*, which means
> a country dweller, and is itself derived from
> *pagus*, the Latin word for village or rural district.
> Similarly, *heathen* originally meant a person who
> lived on the heaths."
> —MARGOT ADLER, *Drawing Down the Moon*

The terms *pagan* and *heathen* have negative connotations
today (though that's beginning to change), but they did not
always. In fact, paganism was merely the way humans practiced spirituality and religion before Christianity existed.
Paganism was practiced by regular people, sparked by the
normal human desires for food, warmth, safety, and survival.
Paganism manifested in ritual and custom like this: If a tribe
was starving and desperate for food, people would act out a
hunting scene using boar skins or similar props, hoping it
would encourage the real thing to happen. It was their way of
encouraging nature in the right direction for the survival of
the tribe.

Over time, these small rituals became symbolic celebrations and tradition for tribal needs and became marked in
the Wheel of the Year (the modern pagan term to describe
the calendar of festivities). The Wheel focuses on the seasonal
equinoxes and the midpoints between each season. These
holidays provide support for all to make it to the next season.
There has been a lot of misunderstanding about these pagan
celebrations. I've heard people joke that they are strange,
over-the-top holidays, but if you understand why they began,

you'll gain a deeper appreciation. Think about our ancestors in the desperate cold of winter, sitting around the fire and dreaming of the sun's warmth. For them, the promise of the future was something to celebrate, and their hope was a tool for survival. Similarly, fall feasts weren't a time to show off to friends or overindulge in food. Instead, they were about using up the final resources from summer before all the food rotted.

THE WHEEL OF THE YEAR

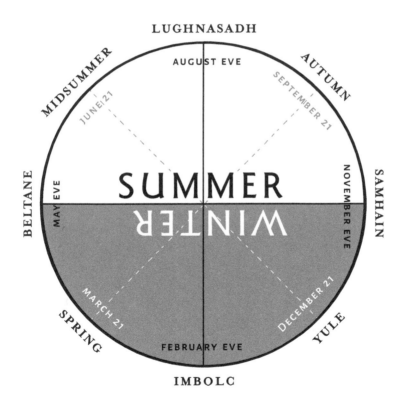

Modern-day pagans still celebrate these holidays to remember where they came from, appreciate the resources that we can access so easily today, and connect with nature. The spell work, rituals, and celebrations that many witches partake in revolve around the pagan calendar. It makes a lot of sense when you think about it: Spells to end things are best done around winter, spells to birth something new should occur in spring, and spells about abundance are most appropriate in the summer and fall.

The Rise of Christianity

In the early fourth century CE, during the reign of Roman Emperor Constantine, Christianity emerged as the dominant religion of the empire. In an attempt to spread the religion, those in charge demonized ancient pagan rituals and traditions. This meant that those who practiced paganism (or other forms of polytheism) became enemies of the Roman Empire. The church began persecuting anyone who engaged in acts that were deemed "not Christian," going so far as putting people to death. This was when the term *heretic* first became popular. Persecution and the hunting of heretics continued for centuries, resulting in hundreds of thousands of deaths.

It is widely believed that early Christians inserted their beliefs into the already-celebrated solstices to make it easier for people to transition from one religion to another. This is why the winter solstice became associated with Christmas and the spring equinox became Easter.

THE MIDDLE AGES

The spread of Christianity and the oppression of other religions continued, eventually triggering a widespread moral panic. Vilified heretics came to be known as witches, who then became associated with Satanic practices because they were perceived as a threat to Christianity. Discrimination among the sexes also increased at this time. According to some historians, during the Middle Ages, attitudes toward women changed dramatically. The idea that women were weaker and more susceptible to the devil's persuasion than men became prevalent. It didn't take long for these cultural fears to insert themselves into laws and the judicial system. In 1022 King Robert of France approved trials against over a dozen individuals accused of practicing religious heresy. This was the first time anyone was put on trial for being "against Christianity."

About 200 years later, Pope Gregory IX decreed that individuals who refused to practice the "correct" faith were to be executed. These laws not only gave substance to widespread fears of corruption by the devil but also sanctioned killing people over it.

When people talk about early witch hunts, one of the first stories that springs to mind is that of Alice Kyteler. She was one of the first people to be condemned for witchcraft and the very first in Ireland. Alice Kyteler was a wealthy woman who happened to outlive several husbands. Life expectancy wasn't very high in those days, so this really was not very unusual. However, a woman with money and power without a man to control her was enough to start the rumor mill going. She was charged with witchcraft and accused of practicing dark arts with her girlfriends. It was even claimed that she had intercourse with demons. A rich single woman with lots of cohorts and demon lovers? These were not the type of rumors the church was going to ignore. She also allegedly used spells to conjure up evil spirits. All of this eventually led to her trial, which in turn led to the trials of at least 11 others who were close to Kyteler. Kyteler was found guilty, but the night before she was supposed to be killed, she escaped.

As anyone would expect, these trials triggered a snowball effect that culminated in the Burning Times.

THE BURNING TIMES AND WHAT LED UP TO THEM

The Burning Times was the period between the fifteenth and eighteenth centuries when thousands of witch trials and witch burnings took place across Europe.

In 1486, a book called *Malleus Maleficarum*—translated as the *Hammer of Witches*—by Heinrich Kramer and Jacob Sprenger was published. This book was the primary guide to finding and torturing witches. It was a bestselling book of its time, second only to the Bible in terms of sales for almost 200 years. Just like Stephenie Meyer's *Twilight*, *Malleus Maleficarum* captured the public's imagination. It was even used by royal courts to prosecute witches during the sixteenth and seventeenth centuries. To this day, it still serves as the foundation for the majority of superstitions against witches.

The exact figures are hard to know, but it is believed that 200,000 to 500,000 people were executed in Europe during the Burning Times, and 85 percent of those executed were women.

THE SALEM WITCH TRIALS

In 1692, over two hundred people were accused of practicing witchcraft in colonial Massachusetts. Nineteen were found guilty—fourteen women and five men—and executed by hanging. Five others died in custody (one as the result of torture). Since New England was colonized by refugees from Europe who sought freedom from religious persecution due to their own nontraditional Christian beliefs, many people wonder how this injustice could have occurred. It's important to remember that life in the colonies was extremely difficult. A bad crop meant that no one ate, so Puritans were especially susceptible to anything that portended bad luck. It was likely comforting to assume that the bad luck and death plaguing them was due to evil forces, and that it was within their reach to quash Satan's power.

Historical Figures Witches Should Know

Alice Kyteler (1280–?): Kyteler was one of the first people to be tried for witchcraft in a court of law. This led to other trials and resulted in multiple deaths, triggering a chain of events that led to the Burning Times.

Pope Innocent VIII (1432–1492) and Heinrich Kramer (1430–1505): Pope Innocent VIII was the religious leader who teamed up with Heinrich Kramer to start investigating claims of witchcraft. He gave Kramer the authority to start persecuting witches.

Mary Dyer (1611–1660): Dyer was an American Puritan who questioned the church's ideas of worship. She became a Quaker and preached that anyone could communicate with God. The Puritans forced her to leave New England, which she did, but later returned and was executed. Mary's death helped lead to the separation of church and state.

Margaret Murray (1863–1963): Later seen as an icon of the feminist movement, Murray was an academic who studied anthropology, archeology, and folklore. She wrote papers in respected journals about witches and witch hunts. Though some have questioned her work, she became known as the "Grandmother of Wicca."

Gerald Gardner (1884–1964): After the final witchcraft law in Britain was lifted in 1951, Gerald Gardner came out publicly as a witch to spread a new religion (Wicca) that focused on old Celtic traditions.

Margot Adler (1946–2014): Adler was an NPR reporter for three decades. In the 1970s she began exploring Wicca and witchcraft, became a witch, and published one of the most well-researched and respectful books on the subject, *Drawing Down the Moon*.

Present Day

Mainstream society's views on witchcraft really started to change in the 1960s and '70s. Gerald Gardner had presented a new path of witchcraft—a religion called Wicca—that felt similar to the structured religions people were accustomed to, making it more approachable. Shortly after, academics and journalists such as Margot Adler began publicly writing about and talking about witchcraft with respect. With the civil rights movements of the 1960s and '70s already in full swing, witchcraft was seen as a way to rebel against the oppression of society. Witchcraft became a safer space and a vehicle of empowerment for women in particular.

The 1980s ushered in an era of positive portrayals of witchcraft in the media, first with movies such as *Teen Witch* and *The Witches of Eastwick*. Both presented witchcraft in a more positive light than had been seen before. Witches were empowered, intelligent, sexy, adorable—and they were even played by icons like Susan Sarandon and Cher! Witchcraft began to take over mainstream media in the late 1990s and early 2000s. *Charmed*, *Sabrina the Teenage Witch*, *Practical Magic*, *The Craft*, *Buffy the Vampire Slayer*, and others depicted magic as something interesting and desirable.

The Craft made magic feel accessible to anyone. It was powerful for teenage girls to feel as if they could exact revenge on the rapists and bullies in their lives. Then we began to see new, exciting iterations. *Buffy the Vampire Slayer* introduced us to Willow, an intelligent, queer witch who used her powers to fight evil. *Practical Magic* showed us the power of sisterhood, and taught us that ignoring who you are will never bring happiness. While some media representations missed the mark, for the most part they spread valuable ideas. *Charmed*, for example, has been criticized for mispronouncing terms and misrepresenting certain deities as demons. And yet, overall, I would argue that it did a lot of good for the witch movement. It put an end to the "us vs. them" mentality that had long divided witches and mainstream society. For example, one of the sisters on *Charmed* regularly wore a cross while fighting demons off with magic. Just like all of the other shows and movies, it demonstrated that witches can coexist with all.

The biggest shift in modern times is how mainstream churches have begun to view witchcraft. They seem to have gone from deciding to tolerate us to realizing that they have no choice. We made a presence on the scene, and now they can't rein us in! We are lucky to live in a time where, in most places, it's safe to practice witchcraft.

In 2014, the Pew Research Center estimated that between 1 and 1.5 million people in the United States identified as pagans, Wiccans, or witches, and I think it's safe to say that the number has grown since. We now see witches everywhere we turn, both in real and fictional representations. We see witches unafraid to make themselves known—whether it's on Instagram or in real life. Witches and Catholics now gather in coffee shops in New Orleans; Wiccans and voodoo priests come together to share information.

SECTS AND PRACTICES OF TRADITIONAL WITCHCRAFT

Recently there's been an explosion of eclectic witches— witches who do not feel the need to label themselves within a group. In a wonderful way, this makes it harder for people to divide us. We're becoming one big, wonderful, unique, magical melting pot of goodness. That said, if you are interested in Wicca and traditional witchcraft, there are a few different groups you can research:

∴ **Gardnerian Wicca:** As we've discussed, in the 1950s, Gerald Gardner brought Wicca into the public eye when the last of the witchcraft laws in England were lifted. He claimed to have been initiated as a Wiccan in the 1930s. He started his own sect called Gardnerian Wicca, which is typically organized into covens. Within the covens, there are hierarchical positions of High Priest and High Priestess. Gardnerians also celebrate a God and Goddess, and rituals are typically kept secret from nonmembers of the tradition.

∴ **Feri Tradition:** Founded in the 1960s by Victor and Cora Anderson, the Feri Tradition came about in California. This tradition has a focus on sensuality and the spiritual care of both body and soul. It also has more flexibility than some other traditions in regard to members' gender identity and sexuality, which many felt was needed within the Wiccan community at the time this branch was founded. Witches within this practice adopt beliefs from many other religions and cultural traditions, incorporating things as diverse as Christian mythology, conjure work, and Greek mythology, among others.

∴ **Alexandrian Wicca:** Founded by Alex and Maxine Sanders in the 1960s, Alexandrian practices focus on the polarity of male and female energies. With a heavy emphasis on ceremonial magic, the coven is an important (and required) aspect of this tradition. To be a part of the Alexandrian tradition, one must be initiated, and members work within a degree ranking. Similar to Gardnerian Wicca, there is some secrecy about its unique practices among members.

∴ **Dianic Wicca:** Named after the Roman goddess Diana, this tradition is different from the ones above because adherents only worship the goddesses and not a god. Typically, Dianic covens are women only. Dianic Wicca has adopted other traditions from the practices above, as well as incorporated folk magic that is typically found outside of traditional Wiccan practices.

CHAPTER **2**

CORE BELIEFS AND VALUES

Now that you have a foundation of history, we can delve into the core belief systems and values of witchcraft.

WORSHIPPING THE ENVIRONMENT AND NATURE

Nature and the environment are deeply important in witchcraft, and that's why honoring them and exploring their wonder are the foundations for many beliefs and practices. The reason nature plays such a large role is that it provides the energy we use in spells, rituals, ceremonies, and spirit work. That energy is the foundation for how all witchcraft, no matter the religion or tradition, is accomplished.

We previously discussed how witchcraft is about the manipulation of energy. In turn, all energy stems from the world around us—whether it's the energy we get from ingesting plants, the energy from a storm that creates physical currents like lightning, or the energy from the sun that nurtures life. Energy is around us and within our environment at all times.

Imagine you are standing in front of the ocean. Feel the breeze entering your nostrils, the salt on your tongue, and the briny smell wafting toward you, and imagine the fresh air entering your lungs. Feel these elements overwhelm your senses. Witchcraft is about capturing that feeling and using the wonders of environment and nature in your life.

Besides energy, nature provides us with many ingredients. Humans have become masters at using the Earth's resources for food and to create medicine, but witches have taken it a step further, finding unexpected and powerful ways to use organic items for magic. Witches often use herbs to create oils, teas, and tinctures, not to mention for more casual things. I've known a witch or two who will readily chew on rosemary to help ease a mild headache.

While it may feel weird to consider animals part of nature (since pets often feel like members of our families), animals are another important extension of nature. Animals often act as companions in works of magic—and they can become totems from which we draw inspiration.

Finally, the weather is a big part of witchcraft. It can be beautiful, but it can also be destructive. Rituals, dances, and chants have been used for centuries in attempts to control the weather. There is great respect for the rain, wind, and sun in witchcraft. Witches will often collect water from a thunderstorm or fresh snow to use in spell work to capture that raw earthly energy.

When it comes to nature, we typically organize the elements into five categories: earth, air, fire, water, and spirit.

Earth is the sturdiest. We know that if we dig our feet into the dirt, we won't go anywhere. It represents stability, healing, peace, **grounding** (becoming grounded), relaxation, and the mother holding us strong against anything that can tear us down. Spells that work with the earth are typically healing spells, calming spells, release spells, and abundance spells.

Air represents our minds. If our bodies are bound to the earth, our minds are free to go where they like. While air is essential to us, it can also be dangerous when it becomes too powerful (think of a strong wind or smoke-filled air). As with our mental health, balance is key. Spells that work with air are spells that are associated with freedom, change, knowledge, and mental health.

Fire symbolizes heat and passion—the thing in the world that keeps us moving forward, that keeps us fighting for what we want in life and for what we believe in. If earth and air are passive, then fire and water are active. They move, they destroy, and they bring emotion to the forefront of our minds. Spells that work with fire are ones for passion, love, movement, intensity, and power.

Water is our emotional element, the one that is all about transformation and expression. Connected to our ability to clean and purify, we use the element of water for creativity and to show the world who we really are. Spells that work with water are spells for transformation, purification, emotion, cleansing, and creativity.

Finally, *spirit* is the thing we cannot touch or see. It is what makes the world so magical and mystical. Without spirit there is no soul, no divination, no connections to other realms and worlds. Spirit is the epitome of witchcraft, and without it, everything else would just exist without meaning anything to us.

CELEBRATING FERTILITY AND SEXUALITY

Sexuality is an important part of witchcraft, both in terms of the fertility of the Earth and the bodies of witches themselves. Exploring sexuality and organic cycles is key to understanding what is sacred in witchcraft.

The Fertility of the Earth

We witness the Earth's ability to rebirth itself every year. We see the transition from frozen in the winter to growth in spring. People have been in awe of this basic form of resurrection for as long as we've been around. Witches, too, are in awe. We have found ways to harness the energy of this fertile earth, and we actively embrace it within our practice.

The Earth's dirt contains microorganisms that make up almost everything we need for life. The trees that we use to create shelter and the plants that nourish us come from this dirt. Even the blood and bones of our ancestors are contained within this dirt. You can see why the Earth is such a large part of witchcraft. The Earth is the ultimate womb of our known existence. Anything can be birthed from it, which is the inspiration behind many rituals and celebrations.

Human Fertility and Sexuality

Just as the Earth has the ability to create life over and over again, so does the human body. The cells in our bodies die and regenerate, and our bones can break and grow back. The magic we see in the earth's regeneration is the same magic we should see in ourselves. In a way, we are these little walking mini-Earths!

Beyond the rejuvenation that continues our own lives, the female body offers continuous cycles of new life. A woman's womb bleeds at the end of every fertile cycle, and then around 28 days later, a new life is possible. This is truly incredible, even though it's something we often take for granted. Witchcraft makes sacred these acts of regeneration and creation.

Creating life and helping shape that life is magic in its own right, but another aspect is the energy created by our sexuality. Many of us have experienced the palpable energy of being attracted to someone, or feeling someone attracted to them. Likewise, there is energy that is generated during sexual encounters.

Harnessing this energy and using it is called sex magic. With this type of magic, a witch uses the energy that arises during sexual encounters and pushes it out into the world to create change and movement. Sex magic does not have to involve someone else, though—it can arise from masturbation just as much as it can from intercourse or other acts.

The faster the witch's heart beats and the more heightened things become, the more energy is clustered around the witch. The witch then directs that energy toward spell work or toward intentions they are currently focused on.

With sexuality, fertility, and normal human regeneration, we have the ability to create, transform, and reinvent. Witchcraft holds these abilities in high regard and strives to honor them, just as we honor these phenomena when we witness them in nature.

HONORING THE MYSTERIES OF THE COSMOS

The moon is loved by many witches as it is symbolic of our dreams and desires. Working magic around something so beautiful, grand, and just out of reach is a great way to work toward your goals. Despite the moon being a much-loved symbol in the witch community, I'm here to tell you that if you aren't moved by the moon, that's okay. Sometimes new witches I've come across tell me they feel like they have to do moon rituals or they're not being a good witch. This isn't the case.

Even if you don't love the moon as many do, understanding its cycles can be incredibly important to your craft. The moon's phases change from new moon to full moon over the course of each month. When the moon is shifting from new to full, it is considered "waxing," and when it is going from full to new, it is "waning." Many witches who work with the moon will typically do spell work requiring a lot of energy when it is full.

Witches are also invested in other planets within the cosmos, as well as the energy of the greater universe. Because of this, astrology is something that witches often engage in. Witches who are skilled in this practice not only use it as a form of divination, but also as a guide to do spell work. Where certain planets fall can tell you about future events, how smooth an upcoming journey will be, or even reveal personal feelings and concerns.

Connected to the cosmos is the spirit realm, which is where energy exists on a plane apart from ours. This is also where energy imprints. Some believe that this plane is where spirit guides, earth-bound spirits, spirits of place, ancestors, and the lower-vibrational beings exist. Mediums have the ability to go into this realm and not only communicate with spirits but also tap into the energy imprints left behind. Spirit workers use the mysteries of the cosmos and our world to feed and empower their spell work.

TAPPING INTO INTUITION AND PERSONAL ENERGY

Magic is not just about tapping into all of the amazing energy and magical elements outside of us. That is only half of what we should focus on. We cannot forget about the magic within ourselves. This is one aspect that I see many new witches overlook. It's not just about casting a spell for universal energy or moon energy or herbal energy—our own internal energy is an important tool.

Where the Rumors Came From

Broom riding: Ergot is an LSD-like hallucinogenic and potentially deadly fungus that can form on rye. Many believe that women in the Middle Ages intentionally made ointments from the fungus and administered them vaginally with their broomsticks. Though it didn't cause them to literally fly, these ointments certainly provided a high! There is another belief that the image of women riding brooms stems from witches jumping in fields with their brooms to simulate and encourage crop growth, per pagan ritual. Most likely, the combination of these two rumors was too good a tale to fade away.

Devil worship: The myth of devil worship stemmed from the Christian belief that worshipping anyone who wasn't the Christian God was unacceptable. During the occupation and conversion of the Celtic region, Christians found depictions of the horned Celtic god Cernunnos, who they perceived as the devil.

Black cats: The Celts and the Druids loved black cats. They were believed to be good luck, to bring prosperity, and to be good for love. Since these people were considered heathens by the church, their relationship with black felines cast the cats in an unsavory light. This idea evolved when the Puritans claimed the cats were not just animals, but witches themselves taking animal form.

Where the Rumors Came From *continued*

Black hats: The pointy hat wasn't connected with witchcraft until the time of the Puritans. Some said that the devil wore such a hat, so it became associated with witches. Others claim it was actually the invention of the Quakers. It was later adopted by Wiccans as a symbol of **the cone of power** (a method of raising energy within a magical ritual that involves pulling a "cone" of energy up from the earth).

Creating your own power can enhance the magic you do with tools. However, the greater benefit is that once you have created a strong internal power and have learned how to tap into it, you will have the ability to do solely will-based magic, without the use of other tools.

There are quite a few ways to harness energy from within our own bodies. Techniques like meditation, Reiki, visioning, and willpower will allow you to recognize and listen to the energy coursing within you.

TIMING AND CORRESPONDENCES

Almost every subject or element in witchcraft has a corresponding color, day, time, herb, or even food related to it. A lot of witches will use these correspondences as guides in their magic. For example, do you want to perform a love spell? Well, the best way to do it is to gather the power of all that corresponds—use a pink candle rolled in dried roses on a Friday with a full or waxing moon, while channeling the Norse goddess of love and beauty.

Learning about correspondences is easy—there are lists devoted to this. For the sake of space, I am not going to note them all here, but many can be found written out in spell books. When you are starting out, these types of guides are immensely helpful.

Of course, timing and correspondences are also just that—guides. They aren't strict rules of witchcraft. If you can't do your love spell on Friday with the pink candle, it's okay. It's all about energy and power. If these tools help you summon up the energy and tingle you need, use them!

CULTIVATING A MINDSET OF ABUNDANCE AND GRATITUDE

There is a lot of power in cultivating a mindset of abundance and gratitude. When we fill our minds with positive thoughts, it gives momentum to our personal energy and allows us to easily be a force for good, to ourselves and others. Think about it—when a friend walks into the room, beaming with happiness, you can feel her radiating warmth and glowing with energy. Learning how to develop that energy through positive intention is valuable to witches. This is manifested in three key ways:

Have gratitude for the day to day. Being thankful for the small things in life makes a huge difference. Taking a moment to enjoy a breeze, mindfully cuddle with a pet, hug your child and mean it, breathe in the fresh morning air when you walk out the door—this can change an entire day. When you are happy and grateful for the small pleasures in life, your own energy instantly brightens and strengthens.

Understand that there's enough for everyone. Having a mindset of abundance means freedom from pettiness and jealousy of others. When you understand that anything is possible and that there is enough to go around—of whatever you want (money, love, career success, etc.)—your energy will transform into something positive and unbreakable. Weakness comes from stinginess and having a scarcity mentality. Remembering that we are all in this thing together will help you direct your energy to what is important.

Find freedom from others' perceptions: Strive to be your best and to treat others well, but remember that after you've done that, you aren't responsible for others' insecurities or ill will toward you. Being genuinely free from others' perceptions and reactions is powerful. You are an independent and strong witch, and freeing yourself from the negative energy others put out will create a lot of real estate in your mind for your spiritual practices.

HEALING AND HELPING OTHERS

We live in a very individualistic society where we are focused on our own care and well-being. While this is ideal for developing our own growth and happiness, we sometimes just *forget* about other people. It may not be malicious or ill-willed, but we're just busy or distracted. Remember that doing something good for someone else does not take away from you. (Abundance mentality!) If you have the skill and ability to help others, why not use it? Helping other witches grow and develop, assisting non-witches, and using spell work to clear paths for others— these are all values in witchcraft. Be a conductor for positive energy. You may be shocked to see a chain reaction: When you help make the world easy for others, suddenly the world gets easier for you, too.

Are we responsible for the well-being of *everyone* in our lives? This is a question I've seen many witches struggle with. When we do spell work to help a friend get a job, heal a coworker from an injury, or create a peaceful environment, we give our time, heart, energy, and magic to the cause. Our instincts tell us to save the world, but remember that we all have our limits. The time you spend helping those who are ungrateful or resistant to change takes time away from helping others who would benefit from your assistance. So much of our power comes from our ability to choose who we interact with and who we avoid. Energy is a powerful thing, so when it's time to give yours away to others, choose wisely.

BREAKING DOWN THE IDEA OF GOOD VS. EVIL

"True magic is neither black, nor white—it's both because nature is both. Loving and cruel, all at the same time."
—LIRIO, *The Craft*

White magic, black magic; white witches, grey witches; good magic, evil magic. As you explore your magical path, you will start to hear terms like these. The truth is that trying to classify something as purely good or purely bad lacks empathy and complex thought. In witchcraft there are no absolutes—nothing is inherently good or bad.

If that's the case, how do you know if you're making the right choice when doing a spell? Intuition. Follow your gut and your moral compass about what is right and what is not. Just because you've made mistakes doesn't mean you're "evil," and just because you've done something for someone else doesn't mean you're "good." Try to throw those labels out. It all comes down to trusting yourself and thinking through actions and consequences. If you decide to do a spell to keep an abusive boyfriend away from a dear friend, some people may view that as controlling an individual's will, making it "bad" witchcraft. But if you feel that's your best course of action and you've thought it through, you can be at peace making that choice. Sometimes there is a good reason to hex someone, and that doesn't mean you're "evil." What is the point of working so hard to curate this power if we can't use it in tough situations? You alone have the right to judge why you may or may not do certain spells.

Many witches do believe that the spell work you perform has an effect on the universe and that everything balances out. A spell that is justified is one you don't have to worry about. However, if you do spells just to create unnecessary chaos, the universe might balance out—and not in your favor.

At the end of the day, unless you are a part of a religious tradition that dictates what spell work you do, you have the power to decide what is best for you and those around you. That is what makes witchcraft such an amazing way of life: There is no authority to tell you what is appropriate or wrong. You are the witch; your life and your actions are your responsibility.

Stepping Through the Door to Witchcraft

When it comes down to it, witchcraft is just the ability to manipulate energy to create change and movement. Whichever way you do that is up to you, and no one can invalidate how you do it. Becoming a witch is a fulfilling journey that entails constant learning and teaching. And ultimately, you get to decide how to use the talents you discover along the way.

Let the universe move you, surprise you, challenge you, and support you—as a witch, your connection to it is mystical and beautiful.

CHAPTER 3

HOW TO TAP INTO YOUR POWERS

Witchcraft is all about seeing the world differently from those around you. Only when you can see the universe clearly can you find your path. I know this is true because I've done it. I've gone from living a life that ruled me to ruling my life, all by tapping into my personal power.

BEFORE YOU BEGIN

When you begin researching witchcraft, you often come across sources that use words and phrases such as *karma*, *intention*, and *free will*. So I think it's a good idea for us to define these terms before we begin.

KARMA A Buddhist belief meaning "the sum of a person's actions in this and previous states of existence, viewed as deciding their fate in future existences," according to the Oxford English Dictionary. You choose your fate depending on your actions: Do good and you will have good karma; do bad and you will have bad karma. Some get so paranoid about karma that they are afraid to take any action for fear of damaging it. If, in your heart, you are doing things with the best intentions, there's no need to get hung up on karma.

INTENTION When doing spell work, your intention is what you're hoping to achieve. Intention is not about the tools; it's about having a clear and concise idea of outcome. Don't be afraid of using the wrong ingredients or not having the right candle—at the end of the day none of that matters as long as your power is flowing and your intention is clear.

FREE WILL Some witches believe that you shouldn't cast a spell if it interferes with someone's free will. I don't follow this rule. Most magic manipulates free will at some level. As I've said before, you are the witch and you have the power to choose what's right for your magic practice.

THE FORCES OF WITCHCRAFT

Witches can tap into energy using divination. We have the ability to feel the energy of the other side to gain information. Some choose to use cards, pendulums, tea leaves, or scrying to assist with this. Others have abilities such as mediumship. If witchcraft is manipulating energy, then those with established psychic abilities are able to tap into this energy a little more easily because they're closer to it. (I genuinely believe that every witch has some psychic ability, which we'll explore later on.)

When we are attempting to create change, we are doing so because there is something interrupting our level of comfort—a need for open communication with someone, a more predictable flow of cash, or the health of a loved one. We feel some sort of issue needs to be resolved.

To understand how to create change, you must understand the sequence of events it entails. The cycle is as follows:

Knowing ⤳ Witchcraft ⤳ Magic

KNOWING Having a clear and concise idea of what needs to change. The first part of creating magic is being aware of yourself, your space, and those around you. A witch may use a form of divination to determine what's going on if they don't already know. They may use cards, meditate for information, or ask spirit guides.

WITCHCRAFT Taking action to create change. It is at this point that the witch needs to determine the best course of action. What you decide to do is based on your magical niche, your instinct about what is best, and what you know about the situation.

MAGIC Change created. Energy shifts and begins to work. Magic typically works from the witch out, into the world.

HOW TO ACCESS YOUR POWER

> "When you start to notice the mystical,
> the mystical will start to notice you."
> —DACHA AVELIN

In this section, we delve into the *knowing* portion of the magical process. Witches often ask themselves: How can I tap into all of this amazing energy around me? Just as there are different elements around us that give off energy, there are many different techniques for tapping into that energy. Let's discuss some ways to access your power.

The Most Common Methods

There are many ways to harness your power and tap into the energy within and around you. The four below are the most common techniques that witches use to conjure internal power.

MEDITATION Meditation is typically done while sitting quietly and letting the mind retreat into itself, forgetting the outside environment and external distractions. There are many different types of meditation that belong to different mind-body-spirit traditions throughout the world. When we talk about meditation in this context, we are talking about using mental focus to get closer to a source of energy. In regard to witchcraft specifically, meditation is a tool for gathering energy. The more "tapped in" you are to the energy around you, the easier it is to put your spell's intention out into the universe. When you're "closer" to an energetic space, your spell's energy can release into the world more easily. It can be hard to explain what this looks like when it's working, but you will feel it. Focus your mind and search for a sort of energetic vibration. When you feel it, concentrate on it and try to make it stronger with your mind. Once you're tapped in, you'll feel as if you have a stream of information and energy flowing between your mind and **the ether** (the energetic dimension often referred to as "the other side" or "the spirit world").

REIKI This is a Japanese technique often used for reducing stress and creating relaxation in order to promote healing. A Reiki practitioner runs their hands around another person's body (or their own) without touching it, channeling unseen life force energy. This manipulation and movement of energy works to balance and heal physical elements within the body. While the focus of traditional Reiki is healing, the technique is used in witchcraft to remove toxic energy from yourself, to move negative energy away from someone else, or to just move the energy created by a spell to where it's needed.

VISIONING Visioning refers to our ability to visualize a future event or scenario playing out. This is a very important part of witchcraft. If we can't imagine our ideal scenario, how will we know the best way to approach it magically? And how will we know if we've achieved our goal? When using visioning, you should picture your ideal outcome playing out in every way, from every angle. For example, if you are doing a love spell, visualize your perfect partner, how you will meet them, what a night in with them will look like, how you will benefit from them, how they will benefit from you, what obstacles are in the way when it comes to meeting them, and so on. Letting your mind sift through these scenarios with intense focus will provide clear direction for the spell you do afterward.

WILL Willpower is probably the most stereotypical idea of how magic works. Basically, it's about using the force of will to get results. While we can't soar through the sky without psychedelics or a plane ticket, willpower is an important skill witches develop over time. The more we get in tune with the energies of the world, the easier it is for us to extract power from them. After years of practice, you'll find you don't need spells to create change—it will simply occur naturally if you put your mind to it. For example, if you have a rift with a friend, you'll find that if you want her to reach out to you, you won't need to do a spell for that. Your ability to work with energy will send that need out into the universe without any effort on your part. The more you work on developing your willpower, the easier tool-less magic will be.

Remember, these techniques will help you get closer to the energy that you are trying to manipulate and change. The more you tap into these energies, the easier your spell work and other methods of witchcraft will be. Keep in mind the cycle: *Knowing* is the first step, when you tap into energy and power. *Witchcraft* helps the energy from your spell work go out in the world with a clear direction. *Magic* is when the change you intended is complete.

Vows of Silence

There are many ancient meditative techniques that people use to gain spiritual enlightenment or to connect with something greater. For instance, Buddhist monks take a vow of silence, people of the Muslim faith practice Ramadan, and Catholics practice Lent.

One popular Buddhist practice is called vipassana meditation, and it is practiced all over the world. Vipassana is the act of self-reflection and self-discovery achieved through abstaining from sex, alcohol, or speaking—all so that an individual can focus on their mind, body, and spirit. In the book *The Naked Witch*, Fiona Horne speaks about a time she engaged in vipassana for 10 days. She meditated for hours every day, did not speak, and ate only vegetarian meals. In the beginning her mind struggled to slow down, but over time she gained an appreciation for things she had never even noticed before. "I was completely and utterly at one with the world and completely at peace. I had no past, no future, no flaws, no hurt—only love. It was better than love. It was ultimate bliss."

Finding ways to shut down a part of ourselves in order to discover something new and connect with the larger energy of the universe is something many witches take on. Vows of silence in particular are a tool frequently used to enhance their perspective on the world and on themselves.

METHODS OF KNOWING THE UNKNOWABLE

Now that you know the basics about how to access energy, we will explore the actions you can take with that conjured energy. Spell work (which we'll explore in part 2 of the book) is one way. Practicing different methods of divination is another, and that is what we will delve into here. Remember, the tools you use to connect to otherworldly energy is personal—do what feels right.

Scrying

Scrying is the act of gaz-
ing into the surface of
an object (a crystal ball,
a black mirror, a body of
water, or another uniform
surface) in order to pick up
on information. The object
serves as a focal point as
our intuition sorts through
information that it's picking up. Scrying should be done in
a quiet, comfortable, darkened area where you feel safe and
protected. I've borrowed my favorite scrying technique from
Kiki Dombrowski's *A Curious Future*. She advises setting up
your scrying instrument—whether it's a crystal ball, bowl,
or mirror—on a table. Light two candles and place them on
opposite sides of your instrument so the surface has a glow
of light but does not show a mirror reflection of your image.
Gaze into the surface. Unfocus your eyes and try to stare into
the void of your instrument. Quiet your mind by focusing on
your breath. Scrying sessions are generally between five and
twenty minutes long. When you first begin, keep your sessions
shorter and continually increase the amount of time you scry.
Don't be alarmed if you begin to see visual images projected
on the instrument or in your mind's eye—this is the goal.

Remember that the images you see will have a special
meaning to you. If you see the image of your pet, it may mean
you need to focus more on your pet, or just that your pet is on

your mind. The images you see from your life or from the spiritual realm aren't the same as what others will see. The more you practice this kind of divination, the better you'll become at interpreting what these messages mean to you specifically.

Palm Readings

Palm reading is a classic form of divination that is very well known. It involves looking at the lines on the hand, the length of fingers, and the texture, color, and width of the hand to learn information about an individual. There are many different schools of thought regarding which hand should be read. Some believe one represents the past and the other represents the future. Others believe you are supposed to always read the dominant hand. I personally believe that you should choose whichever hand you feel drawn to in the moment. Set yourself up in a quiet, comfortable, darkened area lit with candles (in the same manner you would for scrying). Take the person's (or your own) hand and study it carefully. Here's what you need to know:

- **Color** signifies health, with a pale or dull color representing possible health problems.
- **Width** signifies strength, with a thin, fragile hand possibly representing weakness.
- A **rough**, textured hand indicates a hardworking nature and creativity.
- A **triangle** created by the lines in the center of the hand suggests a perfect balance of mind, spirit, and body.
- Hand **size** indicates temperament, with small hands representing impulsivity and hasty action.
- When someone makes a **fist**, you can divine the number of children they will have by looking at the lines on the edge of the hand that the pinky creates.

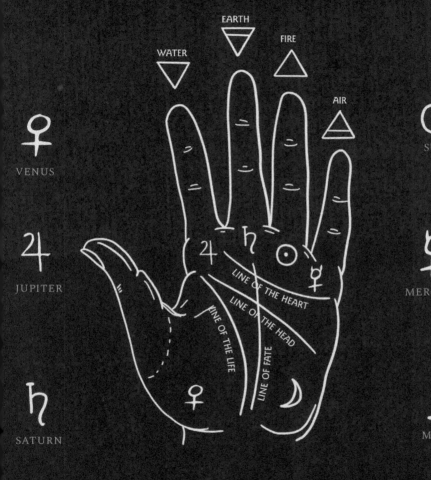

VENUS

JUPITER

SATURN

WATER

EARTH

FIRE

AIR

LINE OF THE HEART

LINE OF THE HEAD

LINE OF THE LIFE

LINE OF FATE

SUN

MERCURY

MOON

- ∴ The **heart line** tells you about an individual's emotional life, and how other lines intersect will indicate when passions are met.
- ∴ The **head line** is a great indicator of career and mental capabilities.
- ∴ The **life line**, which comes up from the base and sometimes through the other lines, is a timeline for how someone's life may play out. It is not set in stone, though.

To learn more about palm reading, and to find out the nuances about how to interpret palms, one of my favorite resources is the book *The Secret Power of You* by Meera Lester.

Card Readings

There are three kinds of card readings: tarot, Lenormand, and oracle. Tarot and Lenormand are set divination systems that are all read the same way, although the artwork on particular decks may differ. The term *oracle* applies to a lot of different cards: herbal, tea, angel, goddess, and everything in between. These are decks someone independently created and defined.

TAROT As a system, tarot is very introspective, complex, and focuses heavily on the **querent**—the person engaging the witch or oracle—and their feelings or actions. The deck has 78 cards, and some readers choose to read reversals to deepen the meaning. Practitioners believe that reading tarot cards helps explore all the depths of the querent's spiritual path. Since tarot is about enriching and discovering a whole new realm of possibilities regarding the inner self, it's ideal for looking within, and is not the best choice when looking at external influences in regard to your situation.

LENORMAND Lenormand is extremely straightforward and looks at the reading from what external factors may be influencing the querent. It is a French system of 36 cards that have simple images with concrete meanings—as opposed to tarot cards, which are meant to be interpreted. Witches who use these cards are able to give very clear readings that have more to do with the issues of everyday life.

ORACLE Oracle cards are much harder to define because every single deck is different. These are decks that are created by independent authors and artists. These decks will feature images important or meaningful to the creator of the deck with definitions created by the author.

Runes

Runes are an ancient Nordic divination system of symbols that are often carved onto small stones, wood chips, or other pieces. Just like any form of divination, you can make your own set or buy them from a specialized shop or online. These are then thrown onto a surface, and whatever symbols appear help divine meaning to the reader. In her book *A Curious Future*, Kiki Dombrowski says that "the names of each of the runes are culturally significant; each rune letter has a name which means something significant to the Germanic cultures who carved them." The most common standardized set of runes has 24 letters and is known as the common Germanic Futhark. It is suggested by many authorities (including Kiki) that you should try pulling one rune a day and contemplating its meaning to become familiar with the runes. Or, try pulling three runes: the first representing the past, the second representing the present, and the third representing the future.

Tea Leaf Readings

Tasseography is the art of reading someone's fortune or future by using the pattern of tea leaves. It traces back to medieval Europe, when fortune tellers would read candle splatters. It evolved in the seventeenth century once tea was brought to Europe through trade with China. Loose black China tea is the traditional tea to use when performing readings.

How to Read Tea Leaves:

1. **Brew a cup of tea using loose tea leaves without any additives (such as spices, dried fruits, or flowers).** When the tea is brewed, pour it into a white or clear teacup.
2. **Once the tea has cooled somewhat, drink it, being careful not to drink the tea leaves settled at the bottom.** Stop drinking when there is about a half teaspoon of liquid left in the cup.
3. **Hold the teacup in your left hand.** In a swift swinging motion, turn the cup from left to right three times.
4. **Carefully place the tea cup upside down on the saucer.** The leftover liquid will fall away and the tea leaves will remain mostly still.
5. **After a minute, flip the cup back over and look at the patterns of the tea leaves.** Try to make out any shapes or forms, and interpret them using a book that specializes in tea leaf readings.

Pendulums

A pendulum is a weight hung from a fixed point so it can swing freely backward and forward. They are often made with chains and crystals, but you can create your own out of whatever materials you like. Witches like to use pendulums to answer yes or no questions—back and forth means no, while a circular motion means yes. Pendulums can be used for other purposes, though. You can use one with a pendulum board, similar to a Ouija board, to spell out words. One folk divination technique is to hold a pendulum over the belly of a pregnant woman to determine the sex of the baby. In this case, a back and forth motion means it will be a boy while a circular motion means it will be a girl. One way to practice using a pendulum is to read for a friend and ask them two questions (only one that they know the answer to). If the pendulum answers the control question correctly, you know it's working.

Ouija Boards

A Ouija board is a flat board marked with the letters of the alphabet, the numerals 0–9, the words *yes, no, hello* (occasionally), and *goodbye*, along with various symbols and graphics. It uses a small heart-shaped piece of wood or plastic called a planchette. Participants place their fingers on the planchette, and it is moved about the board to spell out words and communicate messages. While Ouija boards originally gained popularity during the spiritualism movement of the late nineteenth century, they eventually fell out of fashion. However, after the 1973 film *The Exorcist,* these boards gained a new, less respected reputation as a spooky game for kids. I am of the belief that Ouija boards are just as powerful as any other form of divination. If you go through the processes we've talked about in this book, learning how to control your power and energy, you shouldn't have any problems when it comes to using these tools. Just be smart and protect yourself.

Protecting Yourself

When it comes to tapping into all of this amazing power, we have to accept that we may run into energy we don't like. Energy that may be thick, negative, or just overall icky. You'll know you're encountering bad energy because . . . well, it feels bad. It may make you feel on edge or uneasy.

Here are some great techniques to fight against bad energy when you encounter it.

WHITE LIGHT This is a wonderful technique that witches use to exert their will over other energy in the environment. It involves sitting quietly and imagining a ball of white light within your gut. As you breathe in, you absorb energy, and as you breathe out, you push this light out. With every breath, you push more light out, until you, your space (and whatever else is necessary) is protected within the light. The more you practice this technique, the better you will get at it. It is best to do this when you feel something negative lingering around but can't put your finger on what it is.

SPEAKING OUT Sometimes the simplest technique is the most effective. If you find yourself faced with an entity or energy that you aren't comfortable with, say out loud, "This is my space, and you are not welcome here!"

HERBS AND CRYSTALS Using herbs and crystals to help protect you and your space is a great option, as well. Do some research to find out which crystals and herbs will best suit your needs based on which you are most drawn to when you see them and which spells you are using. Crystals like obsidian and tourmaline tend to be excellent for protection.

CHARMS, CANDLES, AND FLORIDA WATER Charms and candles are a great way for keeping energy clear and clean.

Using **Florida Water** (a cologne made from alcohol and herbs that's typically purchased from magic shops but can sometimes be found in regular pharmacies in the South) is also a great option. All of these items can also be used to appease spirits.

Other Forms of Divination

There are so many forms of divination such as reading Ogham staves, automatic writing, throwing bones, reading eggs (**oomancy**), reading stones (**lithomancy**), astrology, numerology, and reading flames (**pyromancy**). I won't go into all of them here because I want to keep my promise that this book is intended to guide you through *the basics* of witchcraft. But there is so much more to find out, so if you are intrigued, do some research—it's fascinating stuff. Ultimately the key is finding the system that speaks to you by trying different techniques. Just about anything can be made into divination—candle drops, oil in water, how the moonlight hits someone's face. Trying to create your own system of divination could be a fun exercise.

PSYCHIC ABILITIES AND INTUITION

I believe that everyone is born with psychic abilities. Some of us recognize those abilities and nurture them, while others ignore them. Intuition is our most basic form of psychic ability, and it is the thing that works with us while we use the tools we just discussed. That feeling in your gut, that little voice in your head—these are forms of intuition. We can develop our psychic abilities by using intuition as a jumping off point and directing our intentions so that eventually we have more control.

Our intuition is always running, picking up bits of information throughout the day from our physical and spiritual environments. If you have a feeling you should stop at the store now instead of after work, that you should take a different route to a friend's house, or that you should avoid your favorite coffee shop today, these are examples of your intuition guiding you in your day-to-day life.

Clairvoyance and the Other Clairs

> "Clairvoyance is the ability to see images and
> pictures in your mind."
> —STACEY WOLF, *Get Psychic!*

You may have heard the word *clairvoyance* in association with witchcraft. Indeed, it's an important part of connecting with the energy around us. Clairvoyance is the ability to receive messages from the other side in the form of imagery that appears in your mind. Many people falsely believe that you either have this ability or you don't. In fact, you can work on developing your message-receiving abilities. Some people also mistakenly think that receiving messages is purely passive rather than active. Once again, I'm here to dispel the myth. We're about to discuss how to actively engage and explore the psychic part of yourself, and how to practice developing your abilities.

Many people have heard of clairvoyance because it is the psychic method of message receiving that is most frequently portrayed in the media, but in reality, it is just one type of "clair." There are other "clairs," less commonly known, that fall into the category of psychic abilities. *Claircognizance* means "clear knowing." This is when you just know information without having to learn it from a source. For instance, walking into a room and knowing what conversation had been occurring. *Clairaudience* means "clear hearing" and refers to hearing noises or voices that aren't there, such as hearing your name when no one is around. *Clairalience* means "clear smelling." Experiencing the smell of a passed loved one's perfume when they aren't around is just one example. *Clairgustance* means "clear tasting." An example is if you walked into a haunted location and tasted licorice, only to find out later that it used to be an absinthe bar.

I believe that every witch has one or many "clair-abilities," and knowing yours will help you determine how you best connect to energy, which will then direct your actions as you practice witchcraft. Perhaps you will want to smell an herb rather than taste it, or perhaps you will connect to the spirits by listening for them rather than looking for them.

The best way to determine your unique way of sensing messages is by recalling past experiences. Ask yourself the following questions and let your answers reveal your strongest ability. If you have only experienced a few or even just one of these, that's okay! You can grow and develop your abilities through practice.

1. Have you ever seen the image of something in your mind right before it happens? For instance, seeing what a coworker will wear or even seeing a vision of a spirit. If so, you may be clairvoyant.

2. Have you ever known what someone will say before they say it? Or known what will happen at an event before you arrive? Or known a friend will be late before they text? You may be claircognizant.

3. Have you ever heard a song play in your mind and then found that very song playing when you turn on the radio? Have you heard your name spoken when no one is around? You may be clairaudient.

4. Have you ever smelled the perfume of a loved one who passed? Or smelled the presence of something in a room that isn't there? You may be clairalient.

5. Have you ever sensed a familiar flavor on your tongue and then found out that a friend was planning to cook a dish

with that flavor in a few hours? Or found yourself in an old building that you learn once housed similar flavors? You may be clairgustant.

If you want to develop you clair-abilities, the best way is to exercise them. Try meditating (or doing another form of energy tapping listed on pages 38 to 40), and then imagine what your friend will wear to a party next week if you have clairvoyant tendencies. Or try to hear the song you think will play next on the radio if you are clairaudient. Or try to know what the next text you'll get is if you are claircognizant. Or try to smell what the nightly special at your favorite restaurant will be before you go if you're clairalient. Or try to taste what your friend had for breakfast and then ask them if you are correct if you're clairgustant. Daily exercises will help increase your clair-abilities pretty effectively.

Developing Your Psychic Abilities

Some people are born with natural abilities and talents while others have to work hard to achieve proficiency. Psychic abilities are no different. I like to compare magical and psychic abilities to those of dancers. Someone may be a natural-born dancer, but if they do not practice and develop their skills, a persistent person lacking in natural talent could eventually surpass them. So don't get too hung up on how naturally gifted you are with these skills. Your interest and ability to work hard is really what matters.

I have found that developing your abilities is pretty simple and straightforward. Set aside 10 minutes every day to focus on your psychic clair. Make sure you are in a quiet space where you are comfortable and won't be interrupted. Spend a few minutes meditating before working with the practices that relate to your clair. Try to make some predictions, be open to any messages you may receive, and write the predictions and messages down after your session. If you do this small practice every day and look back on how accurate you are, you'll recognize a lot of growth pretty quickly and be surprised at how far you've developed.

Déjà Vu

Déjà vu is a phenomenon almost everyone has experienced at one point or another. It's a moment that feels like a relived flashback. You may walk into a room or speak to someone and suddenly have the feeling that you've done that exact thing or said those exact words before.

There are several scientific theories surrounding déjà vu. One of the most common theories about its cause is the idea of dual processing—when two cognitive processes of thought that normally work together get out of sync. Another neurological perspective on déjà vu is that it is a momentary dysfunction of the nervous system, or possibly a small seizure, interfering with neural firing. In other words, the current moment is familiar, but we have forgotten why it is familiar. Another theory suggests that déjà vu has to do with attention. For instance, we may get temporarily distracted while we are perceiving a moment, and then once our full attention is back on the present, we may perceive the same moment again, forgetting that we already had an initial reaction to it.

While science is still unsure of how or why déjà vu occurs, some witches believe that it is a form of psychic ability. Some think it is a certain type of vision or that it is the mind experiencing a moment that has, in fact, existed before in some realm.

As you develop and grow, visions and premonitions will begin to come to you more frequently without your prompting. They will come to you in a way that relates to your clair.

Telepathy is another direction you can grow in. If you practice, you may be able to develop a proficiency in picking up on information that others around you are thinking or feeling. It may not be just as it's shown in the movies, but you'll start to notice yourself becoming more in tune with those around you.

Premonitions in Dreams

Visions and premonitions are psychic experiences that allow you to obtain knowledge about an event that you have no way of acquiring otherwise. This could be an event that will occur in the future, one that is currently happening, or one that happened in the past.

Energy has an easier time finding its way into the subconscious when we're at the threshold of sleep. That's why many people find they get visions and premonitions when they are either just falling asleep or just waking up. As you develop your skills for tapping into and manipulating energy, your mind will start to do the work on its own and you will have more premonitory experiences and dreams.

CHAPTER 4

HOW TO PRACTICE WITCHCRAFT

Now that we've gone over how to tap into energy, how the cycle of witchcraft works, and methods of moving energy, we will discuss the tools that are available to you, as well as other practical info you need to know in order to develop your skills. This chapter contains a lot of actionable practices, so try all of them if you like, and make notes in the margins about your results! You never know what will create that spark of power.

COVEN OR SOLITARY?

You may have heard of covens but not fully understood what one is. A coven is a group of witches who practice magic together. Generally, a coven can be made up of as few as 3 people and as many as 20, though the numbers don't really matter since no one has the authority to dictate how people come together—each coven chooses for itself. Coven members will typically practice the same form of witchcraft. Many new witches ask me whether they need to be part of a coven in order to practice witchcraft. They fear that they are not a "real" witch until they join a coven. I'm glad to tell you that this is not the case. Witches can be legitimate when they practice alone or with a coven. We've talked about how personal magic is, so you can see why some may prefer to work alone. Yet others find it profound to be part of a group.

There is an in-between way to practice, as well. You can have a coven that you consider to be your community and that you rely on for support, but you can still practice your witchcraft alone. This is what I do. In my case, years ago I was living in Florida, but my life just didn't feel right. I was getting information from the universe telling me that something was waiting for me somewhere else, so I followed my intuition and packed up my life. I am still part of that coven in Florida, but I practice magic on my own using the tools and rituals that work for me. I don't practice much witchcraft with the coven since I am located in a different state, but we're there for each other when we're in magical need. So, keep this in mind: Solitary does not mean antisocial. Being a solitary witch doesn't make you less of a witch.

The truth is that in modern times, covens are actually less popular than they've ever been. While they are important in some of the more traditional religious witchcraft paths, witches who are non-religious often report that they don't feel the need for them.

Another, lesser known form of community in witchcraft is called a circle. This is a less formal group that gets together to study magic and sometimes celebrate **sabbats** (seasonal festivals—see page 62) together. Whereas covens typically get together on a schedule to perform magic and rituals, circles are much less strict, and members don't have the same kinds of commitments to each other. This is a great option when you're new and still figuring out your personal witchcraft. Members of a circle will not always practice the same type of magic, and there is no formal dedication or initiation ritual, whereas in a coven, there usually is.

Solitary vs. Group Spell Work

Another question I often get from new witches is whether there is a difference between practicing spell work alone and practicing it with a coven. Honestly, the biggest difference is whether parts of the spell are divided up. It is not uncommon for a group spell to be completed by one person—you just do all of the parts yourself. One benefit to a group spell, however, is the different energies and intentions infused within it. This can strengthen your spell. If you want to convert a spell intended for one person to work with a group, give each person ingredients and actions to contribute that will incorporate their energy. However, traditional covens typically have their own predetermined group rituals that work within their belief system.

Issues to Consider When Joining a Coven

Democracy vs. hierarchy: Decide if you want a coven with a leader or if you want a more democratic system in which each member of the coven is of equal importance.

Business vs. family: Decide if you want your coven to be all business or if you want your coven to feel like a family.

Same tradition vs. different traditions: Do you want a coven with members who all practice just as you do (which can aid your spell work)? Or do you want a coven with members that practice different traditions in order to evolve each other's practices?

Large vs. small: The ideal traditional coven size is 13 witches. Can you successfully coordinate 13 schedules for regular ritual or spell work? Decide what size coven you'll do best in—a larger group or a smaller one.

Red Flags

If you are looking for a coven, please keep an eye out for these red flags. In some cases they can mean the difference between joining a coven and joining a cult.

Sex-as-worship covens: Avoid covens that include some sort of sexual act in order to participate or join.

"Cough up the dough" covens: Normal covens run on two forms of financial systems. When the group is small, typically each witch brings what they can. Larger groups will usually have registration fees to pay for events or for yearly coven trips. But beware of any coven that asks for a lot of money or asks often. And be suspicious if it's not clear where the money is going.

Evil eye covens: This is a coven where you notice members are giving each other the side eye. Covens that come with lots of baggage and conflict will be a waste of your time. They've fought with each other before you considered joining, and they'll keep fighting long after you'ved walked away. Drama-filled covens won't benefit you magically.

Mismatched covens: You want to be fully invested in what your coven does. If there's an important group ritual that you're not into, beliefs that make you uncomfortable, or activities that spark no interest, then why get involved in the group?

Flakey covens: If you've been to a few coven meetings and you notice that the attendance is always drastically different each time, that could indicate a lack of commitment among the members.

TRADITIONS, RITUALS, AND CEREMONIES

Many witchcraft practices, such as Alexandrian Wicca, perform rituals and ceremonies to worship and create magic. Some of these groups have ancient beliefs, and witches who participate in them feel that they are tapping into something larger and longstanding. Some say these rituals and ceremonies heighten energy for more effective spell work.

Another benefit to traditional witchcraft is that using worn paths eliminates guesswork. The rituals become familiar and comforting, and they provide structure and predictable results.

Traditional witchcraft offers a solid structure that helps witches build and strengthen their paths, though many witches also report feeling constricted by rules. Remember that there is no wrong way to be a witch; it's about finding what speaks to your soul. So when starting out, try it all and see what fits.

CALENDARS AND CYCLES

Many witches use the calendar to help guide their spell work. This is ideal for witches who feel an energetic connection to the earth, the stars, and the moon. Planning and executing spell work based on these factors helps those witches shape and manipulate the energy they need for their spells. This is also a great way for new witches to start practicing, because the calendar can serve as a little guide from the universe and help with spell and ritual ideas. (Remember that if you're working with calendars, and the moon doesn't resonate with you, don't worry—there are many other paths that you can take.)

Days of the Week

Sunday – The Sun's Day: Some witches will use Sunday for celebrations or to seek joyous energy or for intensely positive spell work.

Monday – The Moon's Day: Some witches will use Monday to do spells that involve divination and astral work.

Tuesday – Tyr's Day: The ultimate day of justice, some witches will use this day to do work regarding court or matters of right and wrong. Others use it as a day of war.

Wednesday – Oden's Day: Some use this day to appeal to the gods and participate in worshipping practices. Money and career spells work well on this day, as well.

Thursday – Thor's Day: A day of family, some witches use this day to do spell work related to the hearth, home, and of course, family.

Friday – Freya's Day: The ultimate day for relationship and love spells.

Saturday – Saturn's Day: This is the day to look up at the stars and do spell work to help with dreams, goals, and desires.

The Seasons and Equinox

"It seems like the usual progression of things: the changing of the seasons affects us on every single level: physical, mental, and spiritual. As nature evolves over the course of the seasons, our frame of mind and spiritual focus follow as well."

—KIKI DOMBROWSKI, *Eight Extraordinary Days*

As the seasons change, the earth shifts and our needs change. Before the days of modern conveniences, humans had to plan strategically about how they would survive different times of year, from the brutal heat of summer to the bitter cold of winter. This led to traditions like swimming in lakes during summer, preserving leftover fruit in the fall, and relying on cured meat in the winter.

In witchcraft, there are more than four seasons—eight, actually—and each has a festival associated with it, known as a sabbat. Each sabbat's celebration is a snapshot of what humans would have been focusing on in the old days in order to make it to the next season. While in ancient times people did not plan and execute the festivals as we do today, celebrating them is a great way to show gratitude for those who came before us. Showing reverence to the ancestors by marking these occasions is important in most traditions. Here are the eight sabbats you should know.

YULE (AROUND DECEMBER 21)

Yule is known as the longest night of the year, when the cold has its dark grip on the world. This is the point when our ancestors would have been most desperate to survive to the next year. Yule represents death, the circle of life, and the transformation of lifecycles. Symbolically, we see the death of the wise crone (the death of plants and life around us) as she passes her wand to the young maiden (hope for new life to spring up). My favorite pop-culture example of this is on the show *Charmed*, when Prue Halliwell dies and Paige Matthews is welcomed.

A witch's favorite things to do during Yule:

∴ Have a bonfire with friends.
∴ Drink spiced wine, and let each guest add in a spice as they concentrate on what they want for the year.
∴ Decorate and burn a Yule log.
∴ Share meals with family and friends.
∴ Use mint, which is the scent and flavor of this sabbat.

IMBOLC (AROUND FEBRUARY 2)

Imbolc is when the cold weather shows signs that it will lift. This is the point where we realize that things will be new again and we can wish away the cold. Symbolically, Imbolc represents moving on and knowing there is a future ahead. We have accepted the death of Yule and await the birth of spring. My favorite pop-culture example of this is from *Practical Magic*, when Sally is able to get out of bed after the death of her husband. Things aren't better yet, but she can finally begin to move forward.

A witch's favorite things to do during Imbolc:

∴ Take time for artistic expression.
∴ Spend quiet time within the home preparing for the new life that will soon bloom back into the world.
∴ Perform self-care for the body as it recovers from the cold.

∴ Reflect on the changes that occurred during the past few months of winter.

∴ Enjoy meditations that take advantage of the stillness of the earth.

∴ Use vanilla, the scent and flavor of this sabbat.

OSTARA (AROUND MARCH 20)

Ostara is when the earth has begun to thaw and the ground is fertile for new growth and ideas. This is the point when we can plant things (literally and figuratively) that we want to flourish, such as flowers and goals. My favorite pop-culture example of this is from *Buffy the Vampire Slayer*, when Willow raises Buffy from the dead. Life is literally crawling out of the ground.

A witch's favorite things to do during Ostara:

∴ Decide what actions will be taken for the rest of the year. Help friends and family create plans as well.

∴ Plant greenery in the earth and watch the sun help the plants grow.

∴ Blow out the insides of eggs and color the outside shells. Then insert slips of paper into the eggs with goals that you want to spring to life.

∴ Use lavender, the scent and flavor of this sabbat.

BELTANE (AROUND MAY 1)

Beltane is the time when all of our planting during Ostara is starting to come to life. Flowers are sprouting, the sun is warming, and color is coming back to the earth. Symbolically, Beltane represents the playfulness of new beginnings, as well as innocence, which is why it's often associated with **the Fae**. The Fae are otherworldly creatures that come into our world through the elements. My favorite pop-culture example of this is *The Witches of Eastwick* character, Sookie, and her ability to grow and harvest crops.

A witch's favorite things to do during Beltane:

∴ Teach young ones about the Fae and make offerings to them.

∴ Take a break from the hard work of your Ostara efforts and enjoy some innocent fun.

∴ Make a bonfire with your friends. You can even do some **fire jumping**! This is a practice that involves jumping over a small fire as a symbolic way of jumping from our mundane world into the world of magic.

∴ Use honey, the scent and flavor of this sabbat.

LITHA (AROUND JUNE 20)

Litha is the midpoint of summer. This is when the sun's rays are strong and intense. Symbolically, midsummer is all about the heat of fire. Your yearly goals should be progressing—you're working hard and playing hard. The heat of fire gives us a reason to get moving and to take action. My favorite pop-culture example of this is from *Charmed*, when Phoebe decides the intensity of her life is too overwhelming and chooses to become a mermaid.

A witch's favorite things to do during Litha:

∴ Appreciate all the hard work you've done this year.

∴ Combat the sun with pool parties and visits to the beach.

∴ Coven bonding time! Dedicate a full day, if possible, to the relationships in your life. Perhaps cool off together with a white wine sangria.

∴ Have a god or goddess ceremony and celebrate yourself, and whoever you're with, as strong beings.

∴ Use lemon, the scent and flavor of this sabbat.

LAMMAS (AROUND AUGUST 1)

Lammas is where we start to see the sun waning and realize that winter will start soon. Food is growing and things are healthy . . . for now. Symbolically, Lammas is all about sacrifice. What are you willing to give up for a spell or for the betterment of your life? My favorite pop-culture example of this is from *American Horror Story: Coven*, when Cordelia has to sacrifice Nan's soul in order to stop the Antichrist.

A witch's favorite things to do during Lammas:

∴ Give up something that doesn't serve you (at least for a period of time).
∴ Bake bread! Bread is a large part of Lammas celebrations since wheat is harvested to create it.
∴ Meditate and be grateful for how fruitful the year has been for you.
∴ Clean house: Spring cleaning gets all the attention, but cleaning during Lammas not only helps you clear out items to sacrifice, but it also prepares for upcoming Mabon.
∴ Use rosemary, the scent and flavor of this sabbat.

MABON (AROUND SEPTEMBER 22)

Mabon is the sabbat when the harvest is complete. The earth is starting to cool down, and we begin making more plans within the home. Symbolically, Mabon is about feasting and the hearth. Start making your home a warm and welcoming place, use up all that leftover fruit, make stews, and prepare to save. Your goals should be coming to fruition at this point, so now it's time to think about saving. A pop-culture example of this is from *Charmed*, when Piper uses her special talent for cooking and keeping her home a warm and safe place for her family.

A witch's favorite things to do during Mabon:

∴ Make jam and fruit pies.
∴ Decide how you will save up the (metaphorical) fruits of your labor from your goals this year.
∴ Plan get-togethers to encourage community. This could be a large meal to celebrate the year.
∴ Give to those who are less fortunate.
∴ Use your favorite fruit—this is the scent and flavor of your Mabon.

SAMHAIN (AROUND NOVEMBER 1)
Samhain is in late fall, and it is the final sabbat before winter comes. The harvests consist of sturdy vegetation like gourds, squash, and potatoes. Samhain is all about appreciating those who have come before us. Symbolically, Samhain is about the dead: We dress like them, we leave offerings for them, and we thank them for all they've done for us. A recent example can be found in the Pixar film, *Coco*. While the Day of the Dead as portrayed in this film is a holiday specific to people of Latinx and indigenous communities, some traditions are very similar to the way many witches celebrate Samhain.

A witch's favorite things to do during Samhain:

∴ Create an altar for ancestors.
∴ Host a silent dinner for visiting spirits.
∴ Leave offerings at a **crossroads** (a place where two roads meet) for lost spirits, since they often wander in these types of spaces.
∴ Use pumpkin, the scent and flavor of this sabbat.

Moon Cycles

NEW MOON The new moon is the first lunar phase, and it is not visible to the naked eye. This cycle is often used as a time for reflection, introspection, and meditation. It's a perfect time to think about what new things can come into your life and what goals to start on. It is ideal for spell work that involves fresh energy or new beginnings.

WAXING MOON The waxing moon is when the moon moves from the New Moon stage and it gets fuller every night. The waxing moon is a great time to work on moving forward, creating a plan of action, or initiate change slowly, over time. Spell work done during this phase requires patience when it comes to forward movement.

FULL MOON The full moon is when the moon is at its fullest point. This is most people's favorite moon phase and is often considered a "good for anything" type of moon. I tend to disagree. The full moon is charged with a lot of energy, which can be overpowering, so it's best to be wise about what spells you perform during a full moon, especially if you are new to the craft. Many witches use the full moon to cleanse and charge tools with energy, which is great. Spell work that requires a blast of energy at once is also appropriate during a full moon. However, spells that require finesse or are a bit more nuanced may be overpowered during the full moon phase.

WANING MOON The waning moon is when the moon is moving from full to new and it becomes thinner each night. This is a time to focus on what you've accomplished, what loose ends need to be tied up, and getting things completed. Reversal spells may be best during this phase because you can use the moon to watch the magic of something dissipate.

SONGS, HYMNS, AND CHANTS

The power of songs, hymns, and chants is palpable and useful in witchcraft.

A song is a lyrical creative expression in which you try to tell a story or create action. A hymn is a song that is specifically a form of worship. With a hymn, you're sending the energy up to be heard by the spirits. This is a form of service and a way to pay homage and show your appreciation to any deities you work with. This is why hymns are so popular in Christianity.

A chant, on the other hand, is a spiritual language meant to transcend worlds and connect everyone. Chants are used to create magic and action. If hymns send energy upward to be recognized, chants and songs send energy outward to fuel workings, magic, and transformation.

How to Create Your Own Song

Songs are like spells, so you put them together the same way you would create a spell. The first thing to think about is your intention. Carefully choose the most accurate and satisfying words that capture your intentions and emotions. From there you can get creative and invent patterns that feel good to you.

Here's an excellent tip from Fiona Horne, a well-known witch and the singer of Def FX, who has used music to conjure magic: "Experiment and find a tone, note, or key (or just a sound) that you really enjoy singing. It's that tone that feels relaxed and fun, that you can really feel vibrating in your chest and mouth. You can happily sing it soft and sing it loud without your throat hurting. Base your chants around this and you will voice them with more passion, enthusiasm, and ultimately . . . power."

WHERE TO PRACTICE MAGIC

When it comes to where you practice magic, remember that the perfect place is the one that gives you privacy to let your magic flow. Don't force a situation that may not give you the ability to let loose. At the end of the day, the space you're most comfortable with will always be superior.

OUTDOORS If you have access to a private, outdoor space where you can practice, you will find some intense magic outside. Water, grass, trees, and open space can be great when practicing. Being able to work within a graveyard can also be useful to witches who work primarily with the dead. Being outdoors affords the opportunity to find a stone or stump to use as a natural altar. You can accent it with natural elements such as flowers, dirt, or water. This is a wonderful, environmentally friendly way to create a fresh altar each time you practice.

INDOORS City witches know that not everyone has access to outdoor space. Regardless, having a private space inside is just as valuable. Working inside does not make your magic less than; you simply may have to work harder to form a connection with nature inside. However, on the flip side, it means you can create a more permanent altar, one with candles and incense that can last.

HOW TO USE ALTARS AND PERFORM RITUALS

Altars and rituals can come in many forms. If you join an established tradition, there will likely be guidelines for creating a specific type of altar and performing particular rituals. If you practice on your own, however, you have more freedom in the matter.

An altar can store your potent energy, and rituals can be created based on how you've learned to generate power. Curating your own way of practicing, and maintaining a personal place to do so can make your spell work easier and more powerful since consistency reinforces magic.

Altars

An altar is a workspace for offerings and spell work. It is meant to be a space that feels energetically charged to you.

The way you set up your altar depends on what witchcraft tradition you choose. If you practice non-religious witchcraft, you can set up your altar based on whatever you like. For instance, you could set it up based on the season you're in, what holiday is upcoming, what spell you're working on, or what god or goddess you like to work with. You could even create an ancestor or spirit altar to gain a closer relationship with the spirit world.

Traditionally, altars are filled with items representing different elements. One common way to create an altar is to use a compass to determine which part of your altar faces north, south, east, and west. You can set it up accordingly: North typically represents earth, so that is where you may put your earth element such as dirt, flowers, or crystals. South represents fire, usually signified by a candle. East is the air, so you can put chimes, a bell, or incense in that space. And west is the water, so a small container of water or salt can be placed in that area. The center is usually saved for an item of spiritual significance or for the focus of your spell work.

As you work through this book, you'll start to pick up on what items feel good in your hands and make you feel powerful. Those are the ones that should take their place on your altar. They have somehow earned a space in your life.

Rituals

Rituals, just like altars, are specific to certain traditions and can be quite personal. However, here is a basic structure you can follow:

1. **Protect**
   The first step in performing a ritual is creating a protected and sacred space (sometimes called "**casting a circle**"). This can be done in any way that makes you feel comfortable. If you have found success meditating, you can do so while implementing the white light protection technique described earlier on page 49. You can create a circle of herbs, candles, and crystals, or you can simply take a cleansing and protective bath with herbs and oils.

2. **Raise energy**

   If you choose to adhere to a specific tradition, there will be a prescribed way to go about raising energy. If you choose not to stick to tradition, you should experiment and decide what works best for you. Use any of the energy tapping techniques we discussed previously on pages 38 to 40 to do this. Some witches will raise energy and power by chanting, by calling on spirits or gods/goddesses, or by welcoming the energy of different elements through words.

3. **Spell work or intention**

   This is when you do your actual spell work by setting an intention for what change you want to occur. You may make a charm, a potion, or an oil, act out certain actions, or simply state what it is you want.

4. **Close the circle**

   This is your release of energy and how you close down the ritual. You're sending away, letting go of, or saying goodbye to the thing you used to raise the energy in the first place. This could be reversing a call to the elements, thanking and saying goodbye to spirits, gods, or goddesses, or quieting your mind and releasing the energy out into the universe to move on from the spell.

Rituals and ceremonies are sacred. If you become part of a tradition, remember to feel grateful for the special ways that you are taught to practice. And if you forge your own path, cherish it.

Spellcasting

As with other types of rituals, every witch has their own unique way of heightening their power before doing spell work. You may find that a certain time of day, a certain outfit, or a certain way you prep increases your power. Try everything and see what works best for you! In the second

half of this book, I will present you with spells, but before
you start experimenting, I want you to understand the basic
structure of spellcasting.

Simple spellcasting ritual structure:

1. Connect to the energy of the world however you would like.
2. Heighten your power by wearing or engaging with whatever makes you feel power surge through your body.
3. Perform your spell using whatever your preferred method
   is—petitions, herbals, folk magic, crafting, oil creation,
   crystals, or stating intentions.
4. Complete the spell and release the energy by either
   grounding, pushing it into the world, or releasing any
   spirits or gods you've called in.
5. Follow through with any actions you've declared in your
   spell work. This could include keeping a charm on your
   body, giving an offering you promised to your spirits, or
   using oils regularly.

CLOTHING AND TOOLS

The media sometimes makes it seem like witches are obsessed
with their tools and their witchy clothing. While it isn't as
extreme as it's represented, the clothing and tools witches use
are important because they're a means of connecting with the
spirit world.

Clothing

If you see someone in robes from any religious tradition,
you're aware that something different and special is going
on. Often certain clothing has specific meaning. Monks
wear robes, nuns wear habits, and so on. Religious witchcraft

traditions are no different—there are rules for what to wear depending on the level of expertise of the wearer or what ritual is occurring. Alexandrian Wiccans, for example, may wear a certain robe the way a Catholic bishop wears a certain hat, but that's just one type of witch. There aren't universal standards and regulations for what all witches should wear, and in instances where there are rules (within specific traditions), those traditions tend to be quite secretive about the meanings of their garments.

Within non-religious witchcraft practices, clothing contains meaning, too. However, most witches tend to wear street clothes when doing magic. Some like to set apart clothes for day-to-day wear and clothes that are specifically—and only—worn during rituals and when performing magic. The most important aspect of any garment worn while practicing witchcraft is how powerful it makes you feel. If ritualistic clothing makes you feel silly or disconnected, you don't need to wear it.

Some witches choose to perform witchcraft naked (known within Wicca as **skyclad**) in order to be completely open and free to the earth and its magic. The idea is to minimize the boundaries between you and the earth and spirits. A naked witch can also be interpreted as a witch with nothing to hide behind: no masks, no gothic makeup, no stereotypes.

If you are an eclectic witch, and choose to forge your own path, the act of choosing magical wear can be really fun. For instance, I wanted a special garment when practicing rituals outside of day-to-day spell work. I spent hours choosing a material that felt good between my fingers that was the right color and even the right level of sheerness. It's now reserved only for when I'm doing important spell work.

Tools

Tools are an important part of witchcraft ceremonies and rituals. Finding the tools that you connect with can take some work. Pick them up, feel their energies, try them out. Use your gut instinct to determine if they should be a part of your practice. I recommend borrowing or buying inexpensive tools until you find the ones that speak to you. Then you can invest in really well-made tools.

ATHAME OR WAND
Athames and wands are meant to act as extensions of ourselves. We hold them to project and direct energy because they help the user visualize and imagine it.

BELL
Bells are meant to alert the spirits. The sharp, vibrating ring transcends worlds and reaches whichever energies, gods, goddesses, or spirits we are trying to contact on the other side.

BROOM
The broom is meant to help move energy around. Many witches do a home cleansing by sweeping their broom across the floor from left to right to remove negativity.

CANDLES

Candles are used not only to represent the element of fire in rituals but also to send the intention of a spell into the air as it burns. Candles can be dressed, anointed, rolled in herbs, used to focus energy, or used as a light source while scrying.

CAULDRON

Cast-iron cauldrons are used as fireproof tools within spell work and rituals. These are great for burning paper, herbs, or incense. I have a small one that I like to use for offerings.

CHALICE

Using a chalice is a way of differentiating the mundane from the magical. As a special cup specifically for use during rituals, a chalice holds sacred liquid to nourish guests or to present as an offering to the gods, goddesses, or spirits.

CRYSTALS

Crystals are solid materials formed by the earth. Many witches use crystals to harness natural energy. Some wear them, some add them to spells, and some use them in grids to create energetic movement.

HERBS AND OILS

Herbs have the double benefit of having magical properties and medicinal properties. You can make potions, elixirs, teas, and tinctures out of them. Magically, herbs can be used to create oils, charms, and other concoctions to move along spell work.

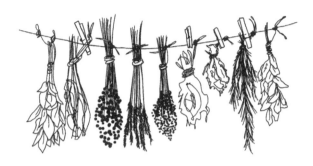

INCENSE

Burned during rituals, meditations, or just for the aromatherapy, incense is used to create a meaningful and sacred space.

STATUES

Statues are used to represent figures like gods and goddesses in spell work, or even animals. A statue helps the witch capture the energy from the entity it represents.

There are many other tools you can use in witchcraft. Watch what others are doing, try it, and see if it's something that works for you. Margot Adler once said that the tools we use are simply props. We use these tools to heighten our energy and power so that we can create magic. Whatever tools you like, either the ones listed here or others, are up to you. Working with items because you feel you have to won't create the outcome you desire if they don't enhance your energy. With that said, feel free to revisit items you once discarded! Just because you decided crystals weren't for you a few years ago doesn't mean they're never meant for you. Witchcraft is forever a journey of magical exploration.

SYMBOLS AND SIGNIFIERS

Like other traditions and spiritual practices, witchcraft has its own terminology and symbolism. I've listed the basics here, but there is much, much more to learn if you choose to dive deeper into the amazing world of symbolism within witchcraft.

Symbols

We all know what a raised flag on a mailbox means or what a cross around someone's neck means. These days, we even recognize the feelings that the emojis on our smartphones convey. Symbols within witchcraft have important meanings as well, and knowing them will help you navigate the world of witchcraft and recognize the work of witches out in the wider world of non-witches.

THE PENTAGRAM AND PENTACLE
The pentagram is a five-pointed star that represents earth, air, fire, water, and spirit. When enclosed within a circle it is called a pentacle. Many witches consider the pentagram and pentacle to be the ultimate representation of their craft. Once you recognize it, you'll start to see it everywhere. It can be found on necklaces, items of clothing, and books of importance.

THE TRIANGLE
The triangle and the **triquetra** are typically used to represent the trinity. Within Wiccan traditions and many others, it is most widely recognized as the

goddess lifecycle—maiden, mother, and crone. Or it can symbolize the more traditional trinity of the father, son, and holy spirit. Still, it can symbolize the past, present, and future.

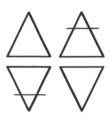

ALCHEMY

Alchemy is usually represented by four symbols associated with the physical elements of earth, air, fire, and water. It can also represent the four elements. Visually these appear as triangles: one regular, one upside down, one regular with a line through it, and one upside down with a line through it.

THE CIRCLE

The circle within witchcraft represents protection and sacred ritual space. Circles mean wholeness, completeness, and energy forever encircling us.

KNOTS

Knots such as the shield knot and similar Celtic symbols represent constant movement forward, and the infinity of life, death, and rebirth.

TOTEMS

Animal totems represent the qualities the wearer associates with a particular animal. For example, if someone has an owl totem, it means they seek to obtain the knowledge and wisdom of owls. A wolf could mean that the wild freedom of wolves resonates with the wearer.

SIGILS

Sigils are symbols that are created in order to capture and house a certain energy or intention. Sigils are created by the witch, using any number of artistic techniques, and can be placed on charms, candles, and other items to create magic.

VEVES

Veves are a group of symbols within a house of Haitian voodoo that represent the astral world and different **loas** or spirits.

Gods and Goddesses

Gods and goddesses do not have to be part of your witchcraft tradition. But some find these figures to be helpful in channeling energy. I encourage you to explore gods and goddesses from all different traditions and areas—and as with other aspects of witchcraft, trust your instincts about what feels right and what doesn't.

How should you decide which gods and goddesses to get to know? I like to think of it as god/dess speed dating! Learn about a few that interest you and see if there is a connection. If so, explore more. If you find that after reading about a certain god or goddess, you just can't seem to get them out of your head, that may be a sign to work more closely with that one.

There are hundreds of gods and goddesses out there for you to research. You can check out Celtic, Greek, Norse, African, Roman, folk, voodoo . . . the list goes on. It's highly dependent on tradition, location, and the magic you like or dislike.

If that feels overwhelming, start by narrowing it down by witchcraft tradition. If you think a free-form type of Wiccan practice may be for you, check out Celtic and Norse gods and goddesses. Or, if you have a connection to hoodoo or folk magic, try exploring African or folk gods and goddesses. You can even work with deities from different locations or traditions that connect to your magical niche if it feels right.

Still unsure? Look at your ancestry. Where does your family stem from? Researching gods/goddesses that have a history in those geographic areas may bring a special connection. In your search, be sure to be respectful of other peoples' heritage, and be careful not to take advantage of a culture that is not yours. Following your gut about what resonates personally is powerful, but being careful about cultural appropriation and practicing with honor is also important.

Names

The use of new names emphasizes the idea of someone being reborn. Once someone joins a coven, they are often given a new name to mark that they are now a new person and are able to leave behind who they were before. Many Wiccans or witches will take on names that involve seasons, animals, and herbals to feel closer to nature or to their practice.

To be clear, you don't need a new name to become a witch or to practice any specific tradition. It's all up to you. Many witches feel they were born witches, and therefore a new name doesn't indicate any significant transition. Their birth name is their witch name. For others, receiving or choosing a new name for themselves can feel powerful.

Alphabets

Known as the Theban alphabet, this alphabet of unknown origins was created in the sixteenth century and adopted later by Wiccans to use within magic, ritual, and spell work. Similar to choosing a new name, choosing a new language can be quite powerful. Many witches keep a **book of shadows**, a place where they keep records of their spell work, private thoughts, and spiritual secrets. Some witches use the Theban alphabet within their book of shadows. Others use the Theban

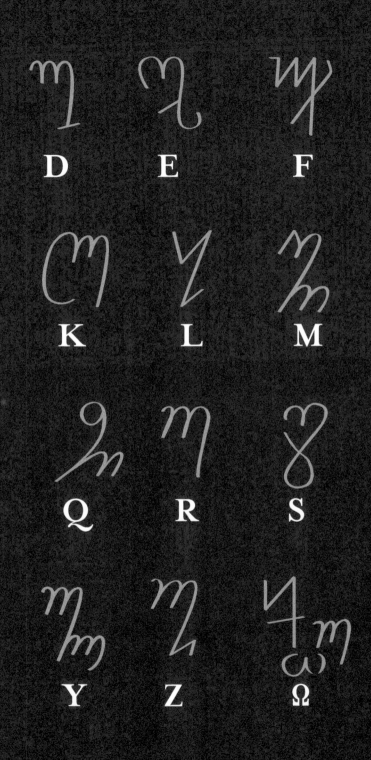

D **E** **F**

K **L** **M**

Q **R** **S**

Y **Z** **Ω**

alphabet only in other works that they want to keep away from the prying eyes of the public.

Colors

Color associations are a way to complement your spells. Remember, though, that magic existed before people dyed candles, so take it all with a (figurative) grain of salt. The color of your pouch or candle will not dramatically change your power, though it could enhance it.

BLACK is associated with reversal magic. The color symbolizes sucking things into a void. It can be used to focus on the unseen, the forgotten, and things that are hidden behind a veil.

BLUE is ideal for healing, calming, and serenity, as it connects to the element of water. It can bring peace to any situation and reminds you to think clearly and rationally.

PURPLE is meant to symbolize spirituality. It can represent someone of authority (spiritual or otherwise). It is also a royal color, bringing prestige and reputation.

RED is associated with love, passion, lust, and fire. Most witches use red for love spells, but it is also a great color for movement. If you need help getting a friend motivated, red will help you light that fire.

HOT PINK is the femme-fatale color. It's a great one to help empower and draw attention. If you have a friend who's looking to get over a bad relationship, hot pink will be the color to bring confidence, sexuality, and power.

PINK is the ultimate self-love and unconditional love color. Pink can represent innocence, pure care, and affection. Pink can also represent children and babies.

YELLOW, the color of the sun, is bright, joyous, and brings celebrations and happiness. It represents abundance and works well in spells about making things a little better. Relationships, friendships, work, or anything else you need a little pep for—yellow's your color.

GOLD is ideal for conducting spells having to do with money, success, or winning. It's the ultimate victory color.

GREEN is the optimum earth color, as it is reminiscent of plants and mother earth. It can help with grounding and growth. Additionally, green has an association with money for Americans, and can represent matters of finance in spell work.

BROWN is the ultimate grounding candle. It can represent letting go of all of one's stress, and being rebirthed and renewed.

WHITE is associated with cleanliness, purity, light, and protection. It is also the go-to color for when witches cannot find the other colors they need. White candles are the ultimate tool. Be sure to have one at all times.

SILVER is another color that works with financial spells. It is also associated with achieving one's goals, but through hard work and dedication rather than luck. Silver can also represent spirits.

PART II

SPELLS

Part I was all about learning as much as possible about witchcraft and magic. In this section, we are going to walk through the door, into the world of witches, and begin practicing spells. The spells here cover the topics of love, health and healing, career, friends and family, spiritual work, and protection.

In chapter 4 we talked about how to do spell work, so here is a reminder of the basic structure of performing a spell.

1. **Connect to the energy of the world however you would like.** Now is the time to make use of the energy tapping techniques we learned about in chapter 3 (pages 38 to 40). Do you prefer visualizing? Meditating? Moving energy with Reiki?

2. **Heighten your power by wearing or engaging with whatever makes you feel a power surge through your body.** Earlier, we talked about setting your space and wearing things that make you feel powerful. Now is the time to implement this. Do you like the idea of a circle of salt and candles? Does a special garment make you feel powerful?

3. **Perform your spell using whatever your preferred method is—oil creation, crystals, herbals, folk magic, crafting, petitions, or stating intentions.** This is where the spells that follow fit into the witchcraft cycle we discussed.

4. **Complete the spell and release the energy.** You can do this by either grounding, pushing it into the world, or releasing any spirits or gods you've called in.

5. **Follow through with any actions you've declared in your spell work.** This could include keeping a charm on your body, giving an offering you promised to your spirits, or using oils regularly.

A FEW GENERAL NOTES BEFORE YOU BEGIN:

1. Some of these spells may not align with the stereotype of spellcasting that you've seen in the media. They may seem too simple or they may seem too complicated. I implore you to come to these spells with an open mind and to use your intentions and the power of your mind to direct your energy and create the changes you desire. Some of these spells involve making charms out of herbs and oils that you carry with you. Some involve making tonics that you ingest, while others involve simmering aromatherapy blends. As I've encouraged throughout this book, trust yourself and do what feels right. Some methods may appeal to you more than others.

2. It's never a good idea to reuse ingredients from your spells that are perishable. Do not reuse food, spoiled herbals, or anything that has been changed by a spell.

I can't wait to guide you through your first set of spells! Let's get started.

CHAPTER 5

LOVE

When it comes to love spells, there are many warnings and words of hesitation out there. It doesn't help that every love spell cast on *Charmed* had odd and dangerous consequences. However, at the end of the day, a love spell is just like any other spell. You're attempting to bring into your life something you're lacking and using a little magic to do so. That being said, it's always smart to be cautious and careful when using love spells.

Quick Passion Candles	92
Charm for Confidence and Self-Love	94
Sugar Jar for Sweet Thoughts	96
Love-Drawing Oil	98
Candle Ritual to Draw Love Near	100
Breakup Forward Movement Spell	102
Attention-Drawing Lustcraft Oil	104
Ritual for Honoring Yourself as a God/Goddess	106

Before we get in to the spells, I'd like to tell you a little story and give some advice. I once dated someone who was *perfect* on paper. He had a great job, we were from the same hometown, he was kind, and we got along. However, there wasn't enough spark between us. I didn't feel that animal attraction to him that I wanted to feel. At the time, I felt like I had to make this relationship work, so I created Quick Passion Candles (page 92) to add a little oomph to our time together. The candles worked very well in the moment. I felt very attracted to him when I used them. But eventually it became exhausting to force something that wasn't naturally there. For this reason, I advise you not to force attraction, love, or fidelity in the long term because it becomes an uphill battle. It's better to spend that time and energy on attracting the right person into your life rather than putting Band-Aids over the wrong person.

SETTING YOUR INTENTION

With all spells it is important to know what you want and to focus on that specific intention. Knowing exactly how you want it, what is in your way, what part you will play in the spell, and how you see your results playing out not only helps you fine tune your spell work and ingredients, but it also makes it clear to the universe what your goals are.

For each spell, set up your space based on what makes you feel most powerful. The essential oils and crystals needed in this section can be found at your local health food store, a metaphysical store, or online.

A BIT ABOUT CANDLE SPELLS

Candles are versatile tools for performing rituals. You can easily create oil and herb blends to add to tea candles or roll onto bigger candles. These are great to store and save for when you need small pops of magic.

QUICK PASSION CANDLES

Sometimes we need a way to generate that spark when we're trying to be intimate. These powerful little pops of magic are great to light during date night with a partner. Full of rose, ylang-ylang, hibiscus, and cinnamon, this sultry scent will become a staple in your bedroom. Why does this work? Rose and hibiscus promote good loving feelings, ylang-ylang promotes lustful feelings, cinnamon provides heat and movement, and rosemary creates a memorable experience. Burning the candles sends the properties and aromas into the environment. I originally published this spell in the February 2017 issue of *Witch Way Magazine*.

WHEN TO PERFORM THE SPELL
Create these candles whenever you feel that energetic rush of power. If you like to perform spells on the day of the week that can enhance their magic, Friday is ideal for most love and romance spells. Light the candles before date night begins.

TIME TO ALLOT FOR THE SPELL
It will take about an hour to create these candles. When using them, they'll burn for about 30 minutes.

WHERE TO PERFORM THE SPELL
Create these in your kitchen and burn them wherever date night takes place.

INGREDIENTS AND TOOLS

12 unscented tea candles
Large pot
About 2 cups water
Stove top
3 drops ylang-ylang oil per candle
2 drops cinnamon oil per candle
1 drop rosemary oil per candle
1 piece dried hibiscus per candle
Sprinkle of rose petals (or hips) per candle
Sprinkle of myrtle leaf per candle
Toothpick

1. Place all of the tea candles into your pot, and pour in a small amount of water so the candles barely float above the bottom of the pot. Do not let the water touch the wax.

2. Heat the pot over low heat and let the candles melt in their tins as you prepare the other ingredients.

3. Add the other ingredients carefully to the candles. Use a toothpick to prop up the wicks as you place the herbs in the melted wax. Feel free to grind up the herbs together beforehand, but put the oils into the wax separately. The wax may overflow, but this is okay.

4. Turn off the stove and let the candles cool for at least 1 or 2 hours before removing them from the water and storing them. Light and use when needed.

CHARM FOR CONFIDENCE AND SELF-LOVE

We don't always feel like our best selves, so sometimes we have to remind ourselves of how awesome and badass we are. This charm will help you feel confident, even during difficult days. Ginger, High John the Conqueror, and honeysuckle aid in personal confidence. Rose aids in loving feelings, and tiger's eye restores personal power. Wearing the charm is a constant reminder that you are an amazing witch.

WHEN TO PERFORM THE SPELL
Create this charm when you start to feel the need for a confidence boost. A full moon is ideal.

TIME TO ALLOT FOR THE SPELL
It will take about 30 minutes to assemble your charm.

WHERE TO PERFORM THE SPELL
Create the charm in a comfortable and powerful workspace, such as your kitchen or your altar.

INGREDIENTS AND TOOLS
1 piece ginger
1 piece High John the Conqueror root
1 piece dried honeysuckle
1 piece dried rose
1 tiger's eye gemstone
Pouch (choose a color that feels powerful to you; red, purple, or pink are great ones for this type of spell)

1. Hold each ingredient in your hand and feel its energy. Take your time as you handle the ingredients. Feel free to add any symbols, herbs, or crystals that aren't on the list but resonate with you.

2. Focus on what change you need to feel in your life, and think about why you are doing the spell.

3. Then, one by one, insert each ingredient into the pouch.

4. Wear the charm on your person—in your pocket, bra, shoe, or any place that is easy and comfortable—for as many days as you need until you feel you no longer need the charm.

5. Once you feel you have your power back and you are finished using the charm, either discard it or keep it somewhere safe as a reminder. Remake the charm each time you feel you need a boost.

SUGAR JAR FOR SWEET THOUGHTS

You may find yourself in a situation where you need someone to think that you are sweet—for instance, when you
want the recipient of an apology to be open to your words.
Or perhaps you are trying to get through a family dinner
with that one cousin who always gives you a hard time.
This jar is a classic folk magic technique. It works because
you're surrounding the person you are casting the spell on
in sugar.

WHEN TO PERFORM THE SPELL
Create this jar a few days before your encounter. Working on a Friday,
Sunday, Monday, or during a full moon is ideal.

TIME TO ALLOT FOR THE SPELL
It will take about 5 minutes to gather everything you need and put
together your jar.

WHERE TO PERFORM THE SPELL
Prepare this spell in your kitchen for easy cleanup.

INGREDIENTS AND TOOLS
Pen
Piece of paper
Small jar
4 cups sugar

1. Write down the name of the person who you need to think sweet thoughts about you.

2. Fold up your paper and hold on to it while you envision your next interaction with that person playing out.

3. Fill your jar halfway with sugar.

4. Place the name into the jar. Then finish filling up the jar with the sugar.

5. Keep the jar in a safe place until you find it's no longer needed. You can discard the jar by either disassembling it and throwing away all of the ingredients, or by burying it.

LOVE-DRAWING OIL

This oil is filled with sweet and spicy aromas to encourage love to come near. Dab a few drops on the bottom of your shoes on a Friday, anoint your candles with it for a spell, or wear it as perfume. Rose and hibiscus bring loving feelings, while ylang-ylang gives us sultry feelings, Road Opener oil helps remove any blocks that are in the way, rosemary is for fidelity, and musk oil is an attractant.

WHEN TO PERFORM THE SPELL
Fridays are known as the day of love, so performing this spell on a Friday is ideal. The full moon or waxing moon are good phases if you want to work with the moon.

TIME TO ALLOT FOR THE SPELL
It will take about 15 minutes to gather everything you need and complete this spell.

WHERE TO PERFORM THE SPELL
Prepare this recipe in your kitchen for easy cleanup.

INGREDIENTS AND TOOLS
Vial or jar with lid
Carrier oil (enough to fill your vial halfway)
1 piece dried rose
1 piece dried rosemary
1 piece dried hibiscus
6 drops rose oil
6 drops ylang-ylang oil
3 drops Egyptian musk oil
3 drops Road Opener oil

1. Take the vial and fill it halfway up with the carrier oil.

2. Add in the dried rose, rosemary, and hibiscus.

3. Next, add in the rose oil, ylang-ylang oil, Egyptian musk oil, and Road Opener oil.

4. At this point you can add in any other ingredients that you see fit, or if you want you can just customize and experiment.

5. Focus on what change you need to feel in your life. Why are you doing the spell? Think about this as you work.

6. Stop wearing it once your goal is met.

TIP Carrier oils are a type of oil that you use to dilute essential oils. Certain essential oils can be too strong to use directly. Popular carrier oils include fractionated coconut oil, almond oil, grapeseed oil, and avocado oil.

CANDLE RITUAL TO DRAW LOVE NEAR

This is an ideal spell to help move possible romantic interests closer to you. Cast this spell when you don't have a mate in mind but are just simply interested in meeting new people. The movers and shakers in this recipe are the red candle, which signifies romantic love, and the pink candle, which represents unconditional love. Bringing these together is ideal for setting up new partners. Using this combination of oil and herbs will pull romantic options close to the witch doing the spell.

WHEN TO PERFORM THE SPELL
Fridays are known as the day of love, so performing this spell on Friday is ideal. Full moon or waxing moon are good phases if you want to work with the moon.

TIME TO ALLOT FOR THE SPELL
This spell will take about 30 minutes.

WHERE TO PERFORM THE SPELL
The place in your house you feel most peaceful—especially a meditation spot.

INGREDIENTS AND TOOLS
1 tablespoon dried rose petal
1 tablespoon dried rosemary
1 tablespoon dried hibiscus
Love-Drawing Oil (page 98)
1 red **chime candle** (see Glossary)
1 pink chime candle

1. Combine the rose, rosemary, and hibiscus in a bowl and grind them into a powder. Lay the powder out onto a hard surface that is easy to clean.

2. Massage the Love-Drawing Oil into your candles, saturating the surface completely.

3. Roll your candles in the herbal powder you created.

4. When you feel ready, light both of your candles.

5. As your candles burn, close your eyes and visualize your ideal outcome. What has prevented you from finding love in the past? Imagine successfully overcoming these obstacles. What qualities does your ideal partner have? How do you see an evening with your ideal partner playing out? What will your partner do for you? What will you do for your partner? How do you imagine meeting this partner? Go over this new scenario from all of these different angles so that your intention is clear. Do this meditation as your candle burns to completion, about 20 to 30 minutes.

BREAKUP FORWARD MOVEMENT SPELL

Breakups can be painful and difficult to overcome. This spell will help you release your connection to your ex. Using fire to release the connection and then water to move forward, you'll find yourself ready for a new chapter in your love life.

WHEN TO PERFORM THE SPELL
A new moon is a nice time to complete this spell.

TIME TO ALLOT FOR THE SPELL
This spell will take about 20 minutes to complete (excluding travel to a body of water, which is optional).

WHERE TO PERFORM THE SPELL
This spell should be done in a quiet and private place.

INGREDIENTS AND TOOLS
1 light blue chime candle
Piece of paper
Pen
Heat-proof container to collect ashes
Body or a bowl of water

1. Sitting in a comfortable space, light your candle and take a few minutes to meditate, focusing on your situation. What do you want to accomplish? How did the breakup occur? What can you do in the future to avoid any mistakes made in the relationship?

2. Write a some words on the piece of paper that define what you want your next step to be. For example, "move on" or "rock my career" or "find an honest love"—whatever you want to focus on instead of focusing on the breakup.

3. Light your paper on fire and say your words out loud. Place the paper into your heat-proof container. Watch as it burns. Watch the smoke linger up into the air, sending your message out into the world.

4. Once you feel ready, take your ashes to a body of water or to your bowl of water. Release the ashes into the water. This will help move your spell forward so that you can progress and transform into who you are meant to be in the next chapter of your life.

ATTENTION-DRAWING LUSTCRAFT OIL

Use this oil when you are ready to draw a little attention your way and add glamour magic into your life. This spell is meant to draw some flirty energy—not a loving relationship. Dab it onto your wrists, clavicle, or behind your ears when you are ready to attract some physical intimacy energy into your life. Rose attracts romantic feelings, black pepper promotes intense attraction (especially in men, so if you don't want to attract men, perhaps skip that ingredient!), and musk is another attractant. This spell comes to us from the ultimate glam witch, Michael Herkes, and it was originally published in the February 2018 issue of *Witch Way Magazine.*

WHEN TO PERFORM THE SPELL
Prepare this oil when you feel your magical energy at its height. As this spell is meant to draw attention, you'll want a lot of power behind it. A full moon may help with this.

TIME TO ALLOT FOR THE SPELL
This oil will take about 10 minutes to make.

WHERE TO PERFORM THE SPELL
Either create this oil at your altar or in your kitchen. This one is all about power, so pick whichever place feels most energetic for you.

INGREDIENTS AND TOOLS
2 tablespoons carrier oil
Small vial or jar with lid
1 tablespoon rose oil
1 tablespoon black pepper oil (test on your skin—this can be an irritant)
1 tablespoon Egyptian musk oil

1. Pour the carrier oil into the vial or jar.

2. Add the rose oil, black pepper oil, and Egyptian musk oil, and swirl together to combine.

3. Focus on what change you need to feel in your life. Why are you doing the spell? Think about this as you work with the herbals.

4. Put it away until you're ready to use it.

RITUAL FOR HONORING YOURSELF AS A GOD/GODDESS

In many traditions, witches spend a lot of time and energy worshipping and honoring gods and goddesses. We give them offerings, perform actions for them, and conduct spells that send them energy. Sometimes our own magical pipes can get clogged. Taking the time to honor yourself and treat yourself as you would a god or goddess by sending healing energy and offerings can be renewing.

WHEN TO PERFORM THE SPELL
Pick a night that is quiet, when you will be undisturbed. Friday nights are a great idea since that is the day of Freya, the Norse goddess of love. Or if you like to work with the moon, choose a night with a full moon or **void moon** (when the moon transits out of one sign of the zodiac and into another).

TIME TO ALLOT FOR THE SPELL
Give yourself a minimum of 3 hours. You don't want to be rushed.

WHERE TO PERFORM THE SPELL
This ritual takes place in various parts of the home.

INGREDIENTS AND TOOLS
Candles
Your favorite flowers
Outfit that makes you feel your most powerful
Bath bombs, bath oils, or bath salts
Favorite pampering tools like face masks or scrubs
Favorite guided meditation audio
Your most guilty media pleasure, like a movie, album, or book
Ingredients to make your favorite meal
Cleansing herbs (for cleansing the space) such as sage, rosemary, or palo santo

1. Begin by readying your environment: Light candles, turn off lights, and set out the flowers. This ritual is about honoring yourself like a deity, giving offerings to empower yourself. Change into your ritualistic clothing—whatever outfit you feel most beautiful or powerful wearing. Slowly gather your bath items, pampering tools, meditation audio, guilty media pleasure, and everything to make your favorite meal.

2. Before you continue, take a moment to cleanse your space with the prepped herbs by burning them as an incense or a **smudge bundle**.

3. If you choose to cast a circle (i.e., establish a field of protective energy and focus around yourself) or welcome in any elements (see page 72), do so at this point. No part of this ritual should be stressful, so take your time and don't rush.

4. Prepare your meal, then eat it.

5. Now is time to start pampering. If you wish, apply a face mask. Run the water for your bath. Add in oils, bath salts, bath bombs, or bubble bath.

6. Soak in the tub and let your stresses and worries melt away.

7. Now is the time to turn on the guided meditation you are using. Listen to it and relax as you soak in your bath.

8. When your bath is finished, dry off and put the same piece of powerful clothing back on.

9. Standing in front of the mirror, look into your eyes and see yourself as a deity. Speak these words: "I am a powerful being, I am a conductor of good and change. I am one to be honored, loved, and respected. May any negative energies sent my way return to their sender."

10. Now that you've been cleansed and have pampered yourself, perform a self-love spell or any other magical workings that feel right instinctually.

11. Continue your ritual by indulging in your favorite guilty media pleasure.

CHAPTER 6

HEALTH AND HEALING (IN YOURSELF AND OTHERS)

In this chapter, we will dive into spells that aid in health and healing. Herbs have real and powerful properties, so do not take them lightly. As you would with traditional medications, please talk to your doctor or a trusted herbalist before ingesting herbs you hear about, read about here, or find online. Every human body is different, so it's important take care of yourself and be responsible. Performing a healing spell is valuable, but that does not mean you should stop taking the medicine your doctor prescribed all of a sudden. Make sure you are well informed about your own health when trying any of these spells. Similarly, magic will not give you instant results. Be patient and let the energy work.

Promote Health in a Sick Household   110

Tonic for Good Health   112

Charm to Promote Physical Healing   114

General Spell for Well-Being
and Abundance   116

Pain-Release Ritual   118

Moon-Glow Oil   120

SETTING YOUR INTENTION

The wonderful thing about taking care of both our minds and our bodies with magic is that we can see a direct correlation between the health of those two entities. The less weighed down the mind is, the easier it is for us to focus on our magic. The less sluggish our bodies are, the better conductors they are for movement and energy. The mind-body connection is powerful. That's why it is important for us to remember that spells cannot undo years of damage or reckless self-care. A 5-minute spell won't make you lose 50 pounds or heal you from a childhood trauma. However, what magic will do is get you started on a path toward healing. A tea of detoxing herbs may gear you up to eat healthier; a ritual to banish past pain may make moving forward easier. The best technique for healing is setting your intention. If you can envision it, you can create a path to the change you want and then use magic to help you on each step of the journey.

A BIT ABOUT SIMMER BLENDS

This simple, easy method is perfect for witches who feel comfortable in the kitchen. Just fill a pot with water and simmer it on the stove with oils and herbs that will help you build strong intentions.

PROMOTE HEALTH IN A SICK HOUSEHOLD

You may find yourself in a household where two or more people are under the weather—especially if you have children. This spell will combat household illness with strong energy. This stove simmer releases healing herbs into the air, unleashing their magical and medicinal properties. Orange and lemon promote uplifting feelings that are much needed when everyone feels ill, eucalyptus is healing—both mentally and physically, peppermint is purifying, while sage and rosemary both have cleansing properties.

WHEN TO PERFORM THE SPELL
When you find yourself nursing a few loved ones back to health.

TIME TO ALLOT FOR THE SPELL
This spell only takes a few minutes to assemble but can be simmered for as long as you like—anywhere from a few minutes to a few hours. Please always keep an eye on your stove while this spell is simmering.

WHERE TO PERFORM THE SPELL
The kitchen is ideal.

INGREDIENTS AND TOOLS
Small pot
Stove top
Water (enough to fill your pot halfway)
1 orange, halved
1 lemon, halved
5 drops eucalyptus oil
5 drops peppermint oil
1 sprig rosemary
A few fresh sage leaves

1. Place the pot on the stove over high heat and fill it half-way with water. Once it starts simmering, reduce the heat to low.

2. One at a time, take each ingredient in your hands in this order: orange, lemon, eucalyptus oil, peppermint oil, rosemary, and sage leaves. As you handle each, feel their energy, and focus on thoughts of healing the members of your home.

3. Add each ingredient to the simmering water.

4. Let the fruit and herbs simmer on the stove for as long as you wish—this spell ends whenever you would like. You may need to add water to compensate for evaporation if you will be simmering the spell for several hours, which is fine.

TONIC FOR GOOD HEALTH

This wonderful little concoction can be taken daily or weekly to encourage and maintain a healthy body and mind. Within magic, citrus always adds good feelings and happiness, so starting your day by giving your body a nutritional and magical boost will make everything just a bit brighter. This spell comes to us from *Witch Way* herbalist Em Miiller and originally appeared in the July 2018 issue of *Witch Way Magazine*.

WHEN TO PERFORM THE SPELL
Prepare this weekly so you can enjoy it each morning. It is perfect during flu season.

TIME TO ALLOT FOR THE SPELL
It will take about an hour to prep and create your tonic.

WHERE TO PERFORM THE SPELL
The kitchen is ideal.

INGREDIENTS AND TOOLS
Juicer
2 or 3 oranges (should yield ⅔ cup juice)
2 tangelos
1 grapefruit
1 cantaloupe
Juice of one lime
Juice of one lemon
1-quart measuring cup
¼ teaspoon cayenne pepper
1 teaspoon turmeric
2-quart glass bottle or carafe with a lid
Water, to dilute

1. Start by juicing your oranges, tangelos, grapefruit, and cantaloupe.

2. Blend all of the juices together in a 1-quart measuring cup.

3. Add the cayenne pepper and turmeric to the juice mixture, and mix well.

4. Focus on what change you need to feel in your life. Why are you making this tonic? What long-term goal are you hoping to accomplish. Think about this as you work in these powerful spices.

5. Once your tonic is all mixed together, pour the juice into your glass bottle. Top it off with water (about 3 cups) to dilute the powerful juice and spice blend.

6. Drink this juice daily to promote and harness the healing magic of these spices and fruits.

CHARM TO PROMOTE PHYSICAL HEALING

We all want to be sick as little as possible. This is a great charm to use if you have a lingering cold or you're trying to speed up the healing of a mild sickness. This spell is about making a charm that contains herbal elements. This will both heal you and protect you from illness while you are vulnerable.

WHEN TO PERFORM THE SPELL
Create this charm after you've come down with an illness.

TIME TO ALLOT FOR THE SPELL
It will take about 15 minutes to gather everything you need and assemble the charm.

WHERE TO PERFORM THE SPELL
Create this charm in a comfortable and powerful workspace, such as your kitchen or your altar.

INGREDIENTS AND TOOLS
1 piece ginger
1 garlic clove
1 piece orange peel
3 drops eucalyptus oil
3 drops peppermint oil
Sprinkle powdered ginkgo biloba
1 small rose quartz crystal
Pouch (choose a color that feels healing to you; white, black, or blue are great for this type of spell)

1. One at a time, hold each ingredient in your hand and feel its energy. Take your time as you handle the ingredients. Feel free to add any symbols, herbs, or crystals not on the list that resonate with you.

2. Then, one by one, insert them into the pouch.

3. Wear the charm on your person—in your pocket, bra, shoe, or any place that is easy and comfortable—for as many days as you need, until you feel you no longer need the charm. Once you're finished using the charm, either discard the elements or bury them.

GENERAL SPELL FOR WELL-BEING AND ABUNDANCE

The busier our lives get and the more stressed we become, the quicker our best intentions get thrown out the window. We may plan to do full-blown rituals to keep ourselves moving forward, but sometimes we end up tempted to put them off "until tomorrow." Before we know it, we've stopped the work. With this spell, I want to give you a practical and easy way to constantly bring good things into your life—in a way that doesn't require you to drop everything. Cinnamon adds a healthy dose of heat and movement, while orange is always good for blessings. Parsley provides a sense of wellness.

WHEN TO PERFORM THE SPELL
Effortlessly incorporate this spell into your normal cleaning routine. If you usually clean on Sundays, for instance, do this spell then.

TIME TO ALLOT FOR THE SPELL
This spell was designed to economize your time and is best performed in conjunction with household chores, so the amount of time you spend on it is up to you.

WHERE TO PERFORM THE SPELL
Perform it in the kitchen.

INGREDIENTS AND TOOLS
Small pot
Water (enough to fill your pot halfway)
Stove top
Half an orange or peel of one orange
2 cinnamon sticks
1 sprig parsley

1. Just before you start your cleaning routine, fill a small pot halfway with water and place it on the stove top over high heat.

2. When the water is simmering, reduce the heat to low and add the orange, cinnamon sticks, and parsley.

3. Let the fruit and herbs simmer on the stove while you clean—or even all day (though you may need to add some water to compensate for evaporation). As you remove the dirt from your home and the things you no longer want in your space, the properties of the ingredients in your simmer will fill the spaces you're clearing out with well-being and abundance. This spell is the perfect way to bring in new energy without the pressure of time-consuming weekly rituals.

PAIN-RELEASE RITUAL

This spell is meant to help release traumas you've been carrying around. It does this by allowing you to symbolically pour your traumas down the drain. This spell was inspired by Fiona Horne's book *Seven Days to a Magickal New You*, because it's all about remaking oneself by rinsing off and releasing yourself from pain.

WHEN TO PERFORM THE SPELL
This is one of the few spells I would heavily recommend aligning with the moon phases: A void moon is ideal.

TIME TO ALLOT FOR THE SPELL
It will take about an hour to complete this ritual, although how much time you choose to spend meditating on past traumas is up to you.

WHERE TO PERFORM THE SPELL
Perform it in the bathroom.

INGREDIENTS AND TOOLS
Small bowl
1 tablespoon activated charcoal
1 tablespoon water
Shower
Lavender oil
Rose oil

1. Start out your ritual by preparing your bathroom as a sacred space. Take time in this space. Meditate on your pain and traumas. What nags at you? What painful events pop into your head? Begin with your childhood and work your way to the present day. This can be an intense process, so make sure you are ready to face these issues.

2. In a small bowl, mix the charcoal and water until you have a thick black paste.

3. Shed your clothing and step into your shower, bringing the mixture with you.

4. Now think back to your meditation, and for every trauma you remember that is stuck to you, mark your body with the charcoal. Each mark should represent a painful memory you are ready to move on from. This can take a while, but do not rush.

5. Once you are finished confronting each memory, turn the water on to a comfortable temperature. Step under the stream of water and watch the charcoal wash away. As the black water drains, feel yourself letting go of the trauma, and allow yourself to feel the emotional weight lifting. This is your chance to start fresh.

6. Step out of the shower and anoint yourself with the lavender and rose oils, representing a new chapter in your life.

MOON-GLOW OIL

This concoction was created to provide you with a healthy glow of post-shower nourished skin. It uses the energy of the moon to do so. The almond oil helps you carry the energy around during the day. It's a relaxing form of glamour magic. This spell comes from Em Miiller, and was originally published in the July 2018 issue of *Witch Way Magazine*.

WHEN TO PERFORM THE SPELL
Create this oil monthly to use daily. If you can create it under a full moon, that is ideal.

TIME TO ALLOT FOR THE SPELL
It will take about 10 minutes to make this oil.

WHERE TO PERFORM THE SPELL
Do this in your ritual space.

INGREDIENTS AND TOOLS
5 tablespoons organic sweet-almond oil
3 tablespoons liquid, organic virgin coconut oil
4-ounce glass bottle with spray nozzle
1 teaspoon silver or golden mica (optional)
20 drops of your favorite essential oil (rose is great for this, but no matter what you choose, make sure it's a non-irritant for your specific skin)

1. Prepare your sacred space as you prefer. You want to capture the energy of the moon, so doing this spell outside under the full moon is ideal.

2. Carefully add the almond oil and coconut oil to your bottle. Stir it gently.

3. Add in the mica (if using) and the essential oil you've chosen. Stir to combine, but do not shake it.

4. Leave your oil mixture in the moonlight to draw its energy. Sit outside with your new concoction, and in your mind's eye, imagine the glow of the moon coming down and infusing your oil. Focus on carrying the power of the moon with you.

5. Take a shower, then apply this oil to your body to promote healthy and beautiful skin. When you wear this oil, feel yourself harnessing the power of the moon as you go through your day or when you tuck in for the night.

CHAPTER 7

CAREER

Spells that aid our careers or financial aspirations are some of the most practical in the world of witchcraft. At some point, any witch is bound to find themselves weaving in a bit of magic to make this stressful part of life more manageable, so in this chapter, I provide you with spells for a promotion, finding work, and establishing a fresh stream of income, among others.

Charm for Finding a Job	124
Success-in-Business Oil	126
Honey Jar for Sweet Words	128
Fast Money-Drawing Oil	130
Ritual to Attain Long-Term Goals	132
Power-of-Three Interview Oil	134

SETTING YOUR INTENTION

While we all wish we could say a rhyme and win the lottery, spells for professional and financial success require quite a bit of effort from the witch casting them. This is because success in these arenas is what everyone craves—both witch and non-witch. Since everyone is always sending out this intention, the witch casting the spell must be willing to really put in the effort to cut through the energy of others.

Beyond that, it can't all be up to the magic—you've got to do your part to make smart decisions. For instance, creating an oil to aid in a job interview will be a nice push, but you must also dress the part, bring your resume, and possess the qualifications needed for the position. The spell can only help those who are logically able to get what they are seeking. The fewer obstacles that the spell has to work through, the more likely the desired outcome will happen.

A BIT ABOUT OILS

Oils are my favorite magic creation technique. They are created with a carrier oil base for dilution. You can throw in essential oils, herbs, and even crystals to create a tiny little powerhouse of magic. Since these spells can accommodate so many herbals and essential oils, they can be customized to any individual situation. I love to use my oils to anoint candles, wear them on the bottoms of my shoes to promote movement, and use them as perfume.

CHARM FOR FINDING A JOB

Any help finding a job when you really need one can be highly valuable to witches and non-witches alike. Wear this charm on your person until you get the job you're looking for. Lucky hand root is the ultimate root for attracting workplace and financial success, and tonka bean can help satisfy desperate cravings for success. Basil and orange oil are classic ingredients for pulling in financial well-being.

WHEN TO PERFORM THE SPELL
Create this charm the moment you know you have to find a new job.

TIME TO ALLOT FOR THE SPELL
It will take about 15 minutes to gather everything you need and assemble the charm.

WHERE TO PERFORM THE SPELL
Create these in a comfortable and powerful workspace, such as your kitchen or your altar.

INGREDIENTS AND TOOLS
1 clove garlic (or just the skin of the garlic if you're worried about smelling like garlic)
1 piece lucky hand root
3 pieces Job's tears
1 tonka bean
1 tablespoon dried basil
3 drops orange oil
Pouch (choose a color that feels powerful to you; green or gold are great for this type of spell)

1. One at a time, hold each ingredient in your hand and feel its energy. Take your time as you handle the ingredients. Feel free to add any symbols, herbs, or crystals not on the list that resonate with you.

2. Then, one by one, insert them into the pouch.

3. After everything is in the pouch, envision your ideal job. Imagine how you'll feel when you get the job offer, as well as the lightness you'll feel knowing you've secured a stream of steady income. Envision how you see the job interview playing out.

4. Wear the charm on your person—in your pocket, bra, shoe, or any place that is easy and comfortable—for as many days as you need, until you feel you no longer need the charm. Once finished using the charm, either discard the elements or bury them.

SUCCESS-IN-BUSINESS OIL

Starting and maintaining a business is very difficult. This oil can be anointed on the doorway of your business, on your cash register or shelves, or on any other tools you use to run your business in order to attract and focus on success. All the ingredients listed below are ideal for monetary success and financial well-being. Plus, spending three weeks feeding the oil jar fresh ingredients infuses it with the care and intent needed to make it more powerful and concentrated.

WHEN TO PERFORM THE SPELL
Wednesdays are great days to work with money magic.

TIME TO ALLOT FOR THE SPELL
It will take about 15 minutes to gather everything you need and complete this spell.

WHERE TO PERFORM THE SPELL
Create this spell in a powerful workspace, such as your kitchen or your altar.

INGREDIENTS AND TOOLS
Silver coin or dollar bill
Glass jar with lid
¼ cup dried peppermint leaves, plus additional if desired
1 teaspoon orange bergamot oil
2 cinnamon sticks, broken up, plus additional if desired
1 teaspoon patchouli oil
Carrier oil (enough to fill your jar)
1 lemon peel, plus additional if desired

1. Gather all your ingredients and any others you'd like to add. The ingredients listed above offer a powerful business success oil, but they can also act as a base, so feel free to get creative.

2. Put the coin or dollar bill at the bottom of your jar.

3. Add in the peppermint leaves, orange bergamot oil, cinnamon sticks, and patchouli oil.

4. Fill the jar completely with the carrier oil before tossing in your lemon peel.

5. Let the oil sit in a dark, cool place for about 3 weeks. If desired, once a week add in additional peppermint leaves, cinnamon sticks, and lemon peels to keep your intentions and goals concentrated.

6. After 3 weeks, you can use the oil.

HONEY JAR FOR SWEET WORDS

Do you need a coworker to say good things about you or show you favor? Maybe it's a colleague who just always seems to be in a sour mood, and you're concerned about how they talk about you to others. Or maybe you have a review coming up and you need your supervisor to speak well about you to the department head. This honey jar will help with those types of situations.

WHEN TO PERFORM THE SPELL
Create this jar when the need arises. A Tuesday would be good.

TIME TO ALLOT FOR THE SPELL
It will take about 5 minutes to gather everything you need and put together your jar.

WHERE TO PERFORM THE SPELL
Create this spell in your kitchen for easy cleanup.

INGREDIENTS AND TOOLS
Small glass jar with lid
Honey (enough to fill the jar halfway)
4 cups sugar (enough to fill the jar halfway)
Photo of the person whom you need to speak well of you
1 tablespoon orris root powder
1 tablespoon cayenne pepper (optional, but recommended if the
    person you are focusing on is spreading hurtful gossip)

1. Fill up the jar halfway with honey and sugar.

2. Add the person's picture into the jar.

3. Add in the orris root and cayenne pepper (if using).

4. Then finish adding in your sugar and honey.

5. Keep the jar in a prominent place in your home while you wait for their communication to change.

6. Once you feel the spell has gone into effect, you can keep the jar in a cabinet or bury it. Do not disassemble the jar.

FAST MONEY-DRAWING OIL

This is my long-standing favorite oil to use when I need some side cash. This is not meant to bring in a stable money flow; it's meant to be a way to get odd jobs that bring in a one-time payment. It's perfect to use when a surprise bill or financial emergency pops up. Wear three drops of this oil on the soles of your shoes.

WHEN TO PERFORM THE SPELL
Wednesdays are great days to work with money magic, but you can also do this whenever you discover that you need some quick cash.

TIME TO ALLOT FOR THE SPELL
It will take about 15 minutes to gather everything you need and make this oil.

WHERE TO PERFORM THE SPELL
Create this spell in a powerful workspace, such as your kitchen or your altar.

INGREDIENTS AND TOOLS
1 tablespoon cayenne pepper
1 tablespoon basil
1 tablespoon cinnamon
Mason jar with lid
5 milliliters patchouli oil
Carrier oil (enough to fill the jar)
1 piece ginger
1 piece lucky hand root
1 piece High John the Conqueror

1. Gather all your ingredients and any others you may have that you'd like to add. The ingredients listed above offer a perfect fast money-drawing oil but can also act as a base for you to get creative with.

2. Place the cayenne pepper, basil, and cinnamon into the mason jar and mix well.

3. Add in the patchouli oil.

4. Fill the jar with the carrier oil.

5. Let the oil sit in a dark, cool place for about 3 weeks. (Note: you can use the oil right away if you're in a pinch, but it's better to let the concoction sit for a while so it can grow stronger for you in the future.)

6. After 1 week, add in the ginger, the lucky hand root, and the High John the Conqueror. This will keep your intentions and goals concentrated and increase their intensity.

7. After 2 more weeks, add 3 drops of oil to the soles of your shoes. Try to wear those shoes until the extra money comes through (but you can take the shoes off when you sleep!), or if you are a freelancer who's seeking a steady stream of odd jobs, make wearing the oil a weekly habit.

RITUAL TO ATTAIN LONG-TERM GOALS

Long-term goals can feel unattainable at times. It can be hard to maintain motivation while working toward something that's so far in the future. This three-day candle spell is a great way to help goals come to fruition because it will help you realize them incrementally and keep you motivated until all the parts come true. Imagining exactly how you see a goal playing out lets the universe know what route you expect it to take. Letting candles burn for a long time lets the energy from your spell release into the environment.

WHEN TO PERFORM THE SPELL
This spell is ideal during a full moon.

TIME TO ALLOT FOR THE SPELL
This spell takes about three hours total—one hour each day for three days.

WHERE TO PERFORM THE SPELL
This spell should be done in a powerful environment where you meditate best.

INGREDIENTS AND TOOLS
1 tablespoon dried basil
½ tablespoon ground cinnamon
Mortar and pestle, or other grinding tool
Small dish
A few drops tonka bean oil
A few drops bay leaf oil
A few drops bergamot oil
1 large pillar candle

1. Collect all of the ingredients and bring them to your most powerful space. Set up your space in a way that you feel heightens your personal power.

2. Once you are ready, grind the basil and cinnamon together—preferably with a mortar and pestle—to create a blend.

3. On a small dish, add equal drops of each oil to create a blend. Massage the oil blend into your pillar candle, saturating the surface completely. Then roll your candle in the herbal powder you created.

4. When you feel ready, you can light the candle. Close your eyes and focus on your goal. What is the long-term goal? How do you plan to get there? What are the steps you need to take? What obstacles are in your way? Meditate on this for a while.

5. When you feel you have meditated sufficiently, you can stop and end your ritual. Let the candle burn until you feel ready to blow it out or you need to leave.

6. Repeat this ritual every night for 3 nights until the candle is burned out. You can discard or bury what's left of the candle.

POWER-OF-THREE INTERVIEW OIL

This robust oil will make you feel empowered and courageous. It's all about combining powerful properties so that you can overcome any obstacle that gets in your way to prevent you from attaining your goals. I like putting it on before interviews. All of the ingredients conjure up confidence, courage, and magical empowerment. This spell comes to us from Kiki Dombrowski and was originally published in the March 2018 issue of *Witch Way Magazine*.

WHEN TO PERFORM THE SPELL
Create this oil when you are feeling your most powerful.

TIME TO ALLOT FOR THE SPELL
It will take about 15 minutes to gather everything you need and make this oil.

WHERE TO PERFORM THE SPELL
Create this spell in a powerful workspace, such as your kitchen or your altar.

INGREDIENTS AND TOOLS
Outfit that makes you feel your most powerful
Small glass vial or jar
Carrier oil (enough to fill vial halfway)
3 drops cedarwood oil
3 drops rosewood oil
3 drops sandalwood oil
3 drops dragon's blood fragrance oil
3 drops juniper berry oil
3 drops oakmoss oil
3 drops vanilla oil

1. Wear the outfit that makes you feel most powerful. Then set up your space in a way that you feel heightens your power. Gather up all the ingredients and any others that you'd like to add.

2. Fill your vial halfway with the carrier oil.

3. Then add all of the other oils in the order listed above.

4. Focus on feeling powerful, courageous, magical, and confident.

5. Dab the oil on your pulse points as a perfume before a job interview. Keep using it during any situation where you feel you need a boost of magic or confidence.

CHAPTER 8

FRIENDS AND FAMILY MATTERS

I've always said there is no point in cultivating a magical aptitude if you are unable to help the people you love. These spells are all about protecting and supporting relationships with friends and family. We are a reflection of those around us, and if we're around friends who are struggling, friends who are in painful situations, or even around toxic friends, it will bring our own energy down. Support yourself, raise up your friends, and you'll always feel blessed.

Candle Spell to Help a Friend
During Emotional Hardship   138

Pizza to Mend Strained Friendships   140

Friendship-Healing Spell Candles   142

Witch Ball for Family Abundance   144

Herkimer Diamond Talisman   146

Freezer Spell to Remove a Toxic Person
from Your Life   148

SETTING YOUR INTENTION

Spells to change the course of relationships often bring up discussions about free will. Some witches believe that no one should cast a spell on someone without their direct permission. So are witches who follow the free will law unable to do these spells? Like I said above, I genuinely believe that being magically skilled is a power and a gift, and if you cannot use it to take care of those in your life, then what's the point? If in your heart, you know you are doing spell work that is good and helpful, don't worry about violating the free will law. Your friends and family are an important support system in your life, so make sure you are secure in your intention before doing spells that involve them.

A BIT ABOUT COOKING MAGIC

Cooking magic is a wonderful, practical, and underrated form of magic. It works the same as any other spell. Think about a wonderful meal you had and all the emotions it contained. Cooking magic works in much the same way. You gather your ingredients, and you work with them to infuse them with magic, energy, and power. The only difference between regular spells and cooking magic is that with cooking magic, you consume the spell instead of throwing it away or carrying it around with you. When you infuse magic into your recipes, those who eat the food will feel what you feel. Anger, love, serenity, euphoria—you can control the emotions of others with cooking magic. It is probably one of the only magical techniques where you can directly and easily control the feelings of those a spell is cast upon, so use it wisely. Note that not every spell in this chapter contains cooking magic, but some do!

CANDLE SPELL TO HELP A FRIEND DURING EMOTIONAL HARDSHIP

This is an ideal spell when you know a friend needs emotional support. A blue candle signifies peace, while a brown candle represents grounding and stability, so bringing these together is ideal for overcoming emotional turmoil. Using this combination of oils and herbs will help bring that friend a little peace.

WHEN TO PERFORM THE SPELL
A waning moon is helpful for this spell. You can also do this spell on a Sunday because the sun brings happiness and hope.

TIME TO ALLOT FOR THE SPELL
This spell will take about 30 minutes.

WHERE TO PERFORM THE SPELL
This spell should be done wherever you feel most powerful.

INGREDIENTS AND TOOLS
Mortar and pestle
1 teaspoon salt
1 tablespoon powdered sage
A few drops neroli oil
A few drops anise essential oil
Small bowl
1 blue chime candle
1 brown chime candle
2 candle holders (optional)
1 bay leaf
Marker
Heat-proof bowl or surface

1. Using a mortar and pestle, combine the salt and sage, and then grind them up to make a powder.

2. Spread the powder out onto a hard surface that is easy to clean.

3. Combine the oils in a small bowl and massage them into your candles, saturating the surface completely.

4. Roll your candles in the herbal powder you spread out.

5. When you feel ready, light both of the candles, and place them in the heat-proof bowl, candle holders, or on a heat-proof surface.

6. As your candles burn, close your eyes and visualize your ideal outcome in your mind's eye. What turmoil is your friend facing? How can they overcome those obstacles? What happiness do you see for your friend? What is the easiest way for your friend to get to this goal? Go over the new scenario from different angles so that your intention is clear. Do this meditation as your candle burns.

7. When you feel done, write the word *overcome* onto your bay leaf with a marker, and light the leaf on fire with one of your candles.

8. Set it on your heat-proof surface, and allow it to burn completely, sending your intention out into the universe.

PIZZA TO MEND STRAINED FRIENDSHIPS

This spell pairs intention-infused foods with a healing environment to mend and strengthen strained relationships. When you sit down with a spell like this, each ingredient absorbs your emotions and energy, infusing them with your intention. When someone else eats this food, that energy and emotion is transferred to them. This recipe was originally published in the September 2018 issue of *Witch Way Magazine*.

WHEN TO PERFORM THE SPELL
When you are having a meal with someone you want a stronger relationship with or when your relationship is in need of repair. Making this with the friend you want a stronger connection with is a great idea.

TIME TO ALLOT FOR THE SPELL
Give yourself a minimum of an hour—you don't want to be rushed.

WHERE TO PERFORM THE SPELL
This ritual should take place in a comfortable space.

INGREDIENTS AND TOOLS
Oven
Baking sheet
1 cup all-purpose flour
Cutting board
1 ball of store-bought or homemade pizza dough
1 cup tomato sauce
1 cup shredded mozzarella cheese
¼ pound cooked ground sausage
½ cup sliced mushrooms
½ cup mini mozzarella cheese balls
½ cup chopped fresh basil
2 tablespoons pesto (optional)

1. As you handle and prepare the ingredients, infuse positive feelings into each one. If you are having trouble, think of a time when you felt joyous and happy.

2. Preheat the oven to 500°F.

3. Place an upside-down baking sheet in the oven.

4. Flour a cutting board surface, and then shape your dough.

5. Layer the dough with tomato sauce, shredded mozzarella, ground sausage, mushrooms, and mini mozzarella balls.

6. Using the cutting board, slide the pizza onto the hot baking sheet in the oven.

7. Bake for 10 to 15 minutes. The cheese should be melted and the edges browned.

8. Remove the pizza from the oven, and add basil leaves and pesto (if using) to it.

9. Share the pizza with your friend in a calm, healing environment.

THE MAGIC IN THE INGREDIENTS

Each of these ingredients has specific energetic aspects:

TOMATO Keeps away negative influences.

CHEESE Raises vibrations.

MEAT Enhances the power of the other ingredients. (But if you want to make the meal vegetarian, removing the meat will not hurt the recipe.)

MUSHROOM Opens up new gateways.

BASIL Turns negative feelings into positive feelings.

FRIENDSHIP-HEALING SPELL CANDLES

These candles are great gifts for your friends. The herbs and oils infused into them will keep your bonds strong and help you mend rifts. When your friend lights the candle, the magical properties of the herbs and oil, plus your own feelings when you made it, will release and create a loving environment.

WHEN TO PERFORM THE SPELL
Friday or Sunday are ideal days, and if you like working with the moon, a full moon would be great.

TIME TO ALLOT FOR THE SPELL
It will take about an hour to create these candles. When using them, they'll burn for about 30 minutes.

WHERE TO PERFORM THE SPELL
Create these in your kitchen, and burn them when you feel your connection to a friend is waning.

INGREDIENTS AND TOOLS
12 tea candles
Medium pot
Water (enough to float the candles in the pot)
Stove top
12 apple seeds, divided
36 drops gardenia oil, divided
36 drops rose oil, divided
Rose hips, enough for a sprinkle per candle
Toothpick

1. Place all the tea candles into your pot and pour in a small amount of water so the candles barely float above the bottom of the pot. Do not let the water touch the wax.

2. Heat the pot on low heat, and let the floating candles melt in their tins as you prepare the other ingredients.

3. Carefully add 1 apple seed, 3 drops gardenia oil, 3 drops rose oil, and a sprinkle of rose hips to each candle. Use a toothpick to prop up the wicks as you place the herbs in the melted wax. (The wax may overflow, but this is okay.)

4. Turn off the stove, and let the candles cool for at least 1 or 2 hours before removing them from the water and storing them. Burn them whenever you feel your friendship needs a boost.

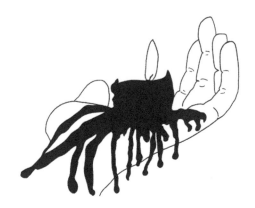

WITCH BALL FOR FAMILY ABUNDANCE

Witch balls are great little ornaments that can be hung around the home. They are little orbs filled with herbs and other items to bring positive energy into an environment. The oak moss in this spell is not only lucky but aids in protection, too. The garlic helps with family togetherness, while motherwort promotes the safety of family. Finally, rose helps with loving feelings, and the olive leaf brings peace.

WHEN TO PERFORM THE SPELL
Create these witch balls on a Thursday. If you can get the whole family involved, that would be fun as well.

TIME TO ALLOT FOR THE SPELL
It will take about 30 minutes to assemble your charm depending on any extra ingredients you add.

WHERE TO PERFORM THE SPELL
Create this in a comfortable and powerful workspace, such as your kitchen or your altar.

INGREDIENTS AND TOOLS
1 handful oak moss
1 garlic peel
1 tablespoon motherwort
1 rose petal
1 olive leaf
Clear plastic or glass ornament

1. Assemble your witch ball by first holding each ingredient in your hand. Feel the energy of each one before inserting it into the ornament. Take time going through and handling the ingredients. Feel free to add any symbols, herbs, or crystals not on the list that are associated with the family.

2. Hang the witch ball outside of the home to bring in positive energy for your family.

3. Remake it every few months, preferably in the company of your family.

HERKIMER DIAMOND TALISMAN

It has been said that Herkimer diamonds have a "crystal memory." Energies imprint themselves in the stone and can be accessed later through meditations and dreams. Because of this, Herkimer diamonds are powerful crystals that can help connect the energies of friends. The following spell is one that you can perform with a friend or group of friends, and it will help strengthen your bond by imprinting your friendship onto the talisman. This spell comes to us from Michael Herkes.

WHEN TO PERFORM THE SPELL
Perform this spell on a Friday that falls between the new and full moon.

TIME TO ALLOT FOR THE SPELL
It will take about 30 minutes to complete, but allow extra time for the candle to burn completely after the spell is complete.

WHERE TO PERFORM THE SPELL
Create these talismen in a comfortable and powerful workspace.

INGREDIENTS AND TOOLS
Small carving tool
1 pink chime candle
1 small Herkimer diamond for each member of your group, or
   1 if you are alone
1 cage pendant for each diamond

1. Carve the name of each person participating in the spell into the candle. Seal it by licking your thumb and tracing your saliva over your carving.

2. Ground, center, and align yourself with the spell's intention to strengthen your bond to the group.

3. Once you are ready, light the candle.

4. Then each group member should place a loose crystal in their left hand. Standing around the candle, join hands so that everyone has a crystal in either hand. Now say the following words:

   Sacred flame that burns so bright,
   Strengthen our bond with all your might,
   Burning strong in love and light,
   May we never part, bound in friendship and delight.

   Focus on the moment and the connectedness you feel with your group, even if you are alone. Think about how wonderful it is to be together. Focus on your memories and how you each enhance each other's lives. These reflections and memories will be stored in the Herkimer diamonds in your hands. Now enchant the stones by repeating the following words:

   Forever together even when we are apart, sealed with the friendship
   inside our hearts.

5. Now place your crystals in the pendant cages, and help each other fasten them around your necks.

6. Allow the candle to burn out completely while your group celebrates friendship.

7. Wear your necklace when you wish to feel close to and connected with your group in the future.

FREEZER SPELL TO REMOVE A TOXIC PERSON FROM YOUR LIFE

This spell is a classic from the hoodoo tradition. It's perfect for removing a toxic person from your life. Freezer spells are controversial since some believe putting someone in the freezer freezes the situation, while others believe it freezes the person out. Try the spell and determine how you would like to use it going forward.

WHEN TO PERFORM THE SPELL
Perform this spell when you are feeling your most powerful. If you like to perform spells on the day of the week that can enhance their magic, Tuesday is ideal for this one.

TIME TO ALLOT FOR THE SPELL
It will take about 10 minutes to gather everything you need and perform the spell.

WHERE TO PERFORM THE SPELL
Perform this spell in the most powerful place in your home.

INGREDIENTS AND TOOLS
Pen
Piece of paper
Knife
1 lemon
Black thread and needle
Black fabric (enough to wrap up the lemon)
Freezer

1. Write down the name of the person you want to remove from your life.

2. Fold the piece of paper multiple times until it's very tiny.

3. Using your knife, make a slice into your lemon and push the paper into the opening. Some witches will add in other herbs at this point that they feel are relevant to the situation and the person.

4. Using your black thread and needle, sew up the incision you made in the lemon.

5. Wrap the lemon in the black fabric and place it in your freezer. Leave it there until the person has been out of your life for a comfortable enough amount of time that you are no longer worried they'll return.

CHAPTER 9

SPIRITUAL WORK

To craft spells that help enhance success and abundance, in this chapter, we will work with and honor the spirits around us. I hope the spells here give you the opportunity to dip your toes into working with the other side. I believe that it's about having a successful partnership with the spirits, so give it a try and see how you like it.

Building a Spirit Altar — 152

Kiki's Flying Witches Ointment — 154

Classic Dreamer's Tea — 156

Petition a Spirit for Assistance — 158

Divination Oil — 160

Spell to Charge an Item with
Spirit Protection — 162

SETTING YOUR INTENTION

When you work with spirits, it is important to be respectful. Spells or rituals that involve spirits typically involve not only an offering to thank the spirits for their help with magic but also a little fuel to help their own energy manifest. Water is the most common tool since it nourishes them. It is also very important to follow through on any promises or deals you make on your end. For example, if you tell the spirit you're working with that you'll donate 10 dollars to a church the next day, you should follow through. Working with spirits is like having a friend or partner on the other side ready to help manifest your magic. Building relationships with spirits is a practice that will become rewarding, and you will find your magic becoming more powerful with the help of friends on the astral plane, as long as you are a responsible partner. When working with spirits, it's important to remember that you are asking for assistance from someone else. Work with love, respect, and caution. Keep a genuine heart when asking for help from the spirit realm.

A BIT ABOUT LOTIONS

Creating topical lotions is a great way to incorporate herbals into your spell work. They are essentially potions that are applied to the skin rather than ingested. Lotions can be created to harness the power of herbs and oils that aid in healing, psychic travel, and glamour magic. If you find you are skilled in kitchen witchery, you may get a lot of enjoyment from creating spell lotions.

BUILDING A SPIRIT ALTAR

Earlier in the book, I explained the elements you can use to build a regular altar. While this is not a spell, building a spirit altar requires many more elements and very specific steps. If you choose to work with spirits on a regular basis, you'll want to do this to keep your connection to them strong. Keeping an altar that is always clean and fresh is the best way to continue a strong relationship with your familiar spirit partners and ancestor spirits. Here is how to build one that you can utilize while performing the other spells in this chapter and any other spirit work you choose to do.

WHEN TO PERFORM THE SPELL
Build your altar during a void moon if possible.

TIME TO ALLOT FOR THE SPELL
Building this altar will take about 30 minutes.

WHERE TO PERFORM THE SPELL
Choose a place for your altar where it can remain permanently.

INGREDIENTS AND TOOLS
Small table
Florida Water (enough to wipe table down)
Piece of cloth to cover the altar
Mirror
Candles
Coins
Divination tools
Small bowl of water
Small plate

ADDITIONAL INGREDIENTS AND TOOLS

Offerings, such as libations, human indulgences, or cigarettes

Items of connection, such as photographs if you knew the spirit when
they were alive, a photo or statue that makes you feel connected to
them, or any items you've worked with in the partnership previously

1. Clean the table where you plan to build your altar. Using Florida Water, wipe down the space and spiritually refresh it. Cover the table with the altar cloth before continuing.

2. Place the mirror and your items of connection at the far back of the altar so that when you work, you can see yourself in the mirror and the items of connection next to the mirror.

3. Place the candles to the left of the mirror and the coins to the right of the items of connection.

4. Just below the candles, set your divination tools. Just below the coins, set your bowl of water. Place the plate in the center of the altar with your offerings laid on top of the plate.

5. This area will be your workspace when you do spirit work. The more you work in the space and the more you nurture it, the stronger and more powerful the connection will become for you.

6. Make a point to always refresh the water and offerings to the spirits whenever it seems necessary. Do not hesitate to sit and speak to the spirits casually in this new space. You have cultivated a powerful space to conduct rituals and spells.

KIKI'S FLYING
WITCHES OINTMENT

This topical ointment is filled with magical and psychic herbs and oils. Applied to the skin, it will help the user with meditation, astral projection, and receiving messages from the other side. This spell comes to us from Kiki Dombrowski and originally appeared in the November 2016 issue of *Witch Way Magazine*.

WHEN TO PERFORM THE SPELL
A full moon or a Monday is a wonderful time to create this ointment. Apply it a few hours before bed to experience messages from the other side during your dreams.

TIME TO ALLOT FOR THE SPELL
Give yourself 30 minutes to gather everything you need and perform this spell. It will also need to solidify overnight.

WHERE TO PERFORM THE SPELL
Create this spell in your kitchen for easy cleanup.

INGREDIENTS AND TOOLS
Double boiler
Stove top
About 5 cups water
8 ounces shea or cocoa butter
3 hazelnuts
3 pieces star anise
3 cinnamon sticks
1 tablespoon mugwort
1 tablespoon dittany of Crete
1 tablespoon cinquefoil
½ teaspoon ground nutmeg (optional, because it can irritate skin)
Large container to hold your ointment

ADDITIONAL INGREDIENTS AND TOOLS

½ teaspoon scullcap (optional, because it can irritate skin)

½ teaspoon wormwood

9 drops benzoin essential oil

9 drops jasmine essential oil

9 drops sandalwood essential oil

Mesh strainer or cheese cloth

2-quart measuring cup

1. In the bottom of a double boiler over high heat, bring the water to a boil, and then reduce the heat to a simmer.

2. In the top of the double boiler, slowly melt your shea or cocoa butter until it is completely liquid. (If you do not have a double boiler, fit a metal or glass mixing bowl on top of a regular pot instead.)

3. Add the herbal ingredients into the melted butter—all except the oils—and simmer for at least 30 minutes, stirring frequently.

4. After 30 minutes, turn off the heat, and stir in the oils.

5. Pour the concoction through a mesh strainer or cheese cloth and into a 2-quart measuring cup.

6. Transfer the still-liquid ointment to your selected container. Allow the ointment to cool and solidify before using it.

7. Use the ointment, applying it to your skin a few hours before bed. Record your dreams the next day. (This practice will train your brain to remember more details from your dreams anyway!)

CLASSIC DREAMER'S TEA

Popularized by writer Scott Cunningham, mugwort tea and its variations have become staples for those who want to work with spirits or receive psychic abilities through their dreams. Brew this tea before bed to help aid in spirit connection and prophetic dreams. Mugwort is the ultimate astral projection and spirit herb, so combined with cinnamon and bay leaf (which also help with prophetic dreams), you strengthen your reach. Hibiscus aids in dream work, too, as does star anise.

WHEN TO PERFORM THE SPELL
Make and brew this tea 2 hours before bed.

TIME TO ALLOT FOR THE SPELL
It will take about 20 minutes to prep and steep this tea.

WHERE TO PERFORM THE SPELL
The kitchen is ideal.

INGREDIENTS AND TOOLS
Small glass jar
1 tablespoon mugwort
½ tablespoon cinnamon
1 tablespoon dried hibiscus
1 piece star anise
1 bay leaf
Medium pot
About 2 cups water
Stove top
1 tablespoon honey

1. In a jar, mix the mugwort, cinnamon, dried hibiscus, star anise, and bay leaf.

2. Fill a medium pot with water, and heat it on the stove over medium heat.

3. When you see the water steaming, turn off the burner and add your herbs. Let the herbs steep for 5 to 10 minutes.

4. Strain the herbs, and pour a cup of the tea into your mug.

5. Add a tablespoon of honey. Drink the tea before bed. This recipe yields about 2 cups of tea.

PETITION A SPIRIT FOR ASSISTANCE

This is an example of how you can work with spirits to ask for assistance. As you work more and more with spirits, you'll learn what offerings they like and which spirit can help with different spells. I like to include donations in my spirit work since I work with the goddess Hecate, the Greek goddess of witches, the dead, and the homeless. Leaving a donation for those in need pleases her, which pleases the spirits.

WHEN TO PERFORM THE SPELL
Do this spell when you are feeling your most powerful.

TIME TO ALLOT FOR THE SPELL
This spell will take about 30 minutes.

WHERE TO PERFORM THE SPELL
This spell should be done in the most powerful area of your home.

INGREDIENTS AND TOOLS
1 candle
Mirror
Bowl of water
Offerings to the spirit, such as libations and indulgences
Donation, such as a $10 bill
Pen
Piece of paper

1. Find a space with no distractions and plenty of privacy.

2. While setting up your space, set out your candle, mirror, water, offerings, and donation.

3. Begin to meditate. In your mind, call out to the spirit you want to work with. If you do not know which spirit you want to communicate with, call out for any spirit of good intent who wants to assist.

4. Light your candle, and make sure you can see both your reflection and the candle's reflection in the mirror.

5. Speak to the spirit, letting them know the offerings you have are for them, as a gift for their time and their help. Then state out loud what it is you need assistance with.

6. Taking your pen and paper, write down a sentence that fully captures your goal, and without lifting your pen, write it repeatedly. Speak it out over and over again as you write. This will help lull you into a meditative trance as you make your intention clear to the spirit, yourself, and the universe. Do this until the paper is full of writing.

7. Once you are finished, state what your donation is. Let the spirit know that you will leave the donation at a crossroads (those in need are more likely to pick up the donation there, but if you'd rather donate it to a church or shelter instead, you can do this as well).

8. Thank the spirit, and let them know your offerings will be out for the rest of the night for their enjoyment.

9. Blow out your candle but leave the indulgences out until the next day before cleaning up.

10. Once your goal has come to fruition, go to the location where you left the indulgences and thank them for their assistance.

DIVINATION OIL

This oil is meant to heighten your divination readings. It can be used in a number of ways: in a diffuser when doing readings, on candles for divination or spells involving spirits, or worn as a perfume when working with others. All of the herbs used here promote psychic development and spiritual connection.

WHEN TO PERFORM THE SPELL
Make this oil on Monday (the moon's day) or during a full moon.

TIME TO ALLOT FOR THE SPELL
It will take about 15 minutes to gather everything you need and make this oil.

WHERE TO PERFORM THE SPELL
Create this spell in your kitchen for easy cleanup, or if you have a dedicated divination space, making it there would be ideal.

INGREDIENTS AND TOOLS
Rosemary incense
Small vial or jar with lid
Carrier oil (enough to fill your vial halfway)
3 pieces bistort root
3 pieces cherry bark
Sprinkle dandelion root
1 piece dried hibiscus
3 drops camphor oil
3 drops jasmine oil
3 drops mugwort oil

1. Prepare your space as you like while burning rosemary incense.

2. Fill your vial halfway with the carrier oil, and then add the dried herbs.

3. Add the camphor, jasmine, and mugwort oils.

4. Add in any other ingredients you see fit or that you want to customize.

5. If you have the ability to let the oil charge under a full moon, it would be perfect to do so. Use it the next time you are performing any kind of divination.

SPELL TO CHARGE AN ITEM WITH SPIRIT PROTECTION

When it comes to protection, my first thought is always to use the spirits. They aid us in divination work and watch over us more often than we realize. Having their protection helps you build your relationship with them but also protects you from spiritual harm. This spell was originally published in in the August 2016 issue of *Witch Way Magazine*.

WHEN TO PERFORM THE SPELL
Do this spell when you are feeling your most powerful.

TIME TO ALLOT FOR THE SPELL
This spell will take about 30 minutes.

WHERE TO PERFORM THE SPELL
This spell should be done in the most powerful area of your home.

INGREDIENTS AND TOOLS
Candles in any color that speaks to you (white is often used in
  protection spells)
Mugwort or wormwood incense (avoid sage)
Item you want to charge (like a ring, necklace, or anything else)
Container of water
Mirror
A few coins
A few human indulgences like chocolate, alcohol, honey, or cigarettes

1. Prepare your space with the candles and incense. Spend some time meditating to get into the right mindset.
2. Place the item that you want charged with protection onto your altar or workspace.
3. Surround the item with the other objects: the candles, incense, water, mirror, coins, and indulgences.

4. Using the mirror, look directly into your own eyes, and state your intention:

    Spirits of goodness and protection, view this item as a connection. A connection between you and I, so that I can always be surrounded by your energy and safety. May only good spirits connect themselves to this object, spirits of harm and chaos are not welcome here.

5. Close your eyes, and using your mind's eye, imagine your item infused with light.

6. Take a few moments to psychically pick up on any messages from the spirit, so you know if they are on board.

7. At this point, speak to the spirit. Let them know that the offerings you have are gifts for them to thank them for their time and help.

8. Taste the indulgences, but save the majority for the spirit. No one likes to indulge alone after all.

9. Thank the spirit and let them know your offerings will be out for the rest of the night for their enjoyment. Blow out your candle, but leave the indulgences out until the next day.

10. Repeat for 2 more nights. Each night, replenish the indulgences and discard the old food and offerings outside in the earth, under a tree, preferably at a crossroads.

11. On the third night, immediately after conducting the spell, take all of your offerings (except the charged item) and return to the spot where you discarded the previous offerings. Once all of your offerings are disposed of, return inside and put on your newly charged item. This shows the spirits that you are ready and confident in their protection.

12. Thank them and repeat this spell quarterly or yearly if you feel it needs to be refreshed.

CHAPTER 10

PROTECTION

Protection spells are at the core of witchcraft—after all, without protection you can't really do much else. Ideas about protection are all around us. Think of the superstitions that have made their way into our culture—from throwing salt over one's shoulder to not stepping on the cracks in the sidewalk. In some parts of the southern United States, there are even homes where keyholes have been placed upside-down to keep entities away. Protection is at the forefront of most people's minds in one way or another, so I'm happy to share a few spells to help you explore protection with your witchcraft practice.

Wearable Protection Powder   166

Weekly Quick Cleansing Ritual   168

Car Protection Charm   170

Clove Protection Spell for Busy Witches   172

A Witch Jar for Protection   174

Hex Breaker Trifecta   176

SETTING YOUR INTENTION

When it comes to protection spells, it is important to remember that they are not a set-it-and-forget-it type of magic. You can't cast a general protection spell and expect it to carry on for years. Why? Because things change. Life changes, circumstances change, threats change, you change. Plan to renew, maintain, and refresh protection magic on a consistent schedule in order to help keep yourself in good standing. Does this mean no harm will ever come to you? Of course not. Sometimes things happen. However, making protection a priority will help keep your path a bit clearer so that you are more prepared to deal with the unavoidable and the unpredictable. When you are working with protection spells, remember to focus on keeping any negativity away from you. Envisioning white light while working with protection spells is one of my go-tos.

A BIT ABOUT CHARMS

Charms are these wonderful little bundles of herbs, stones, and oils crafted into sachets or pouches to correspond to your unique situation. I love these pouches because they are versatile, can be shoved into small spaces, and are ideal for protection magic. My big rule when it comes to charms is to dig deep into your witchy repertoire to make them. Think about the many herbs, oils, and crystals available to you—this will help you look at your situation from multiple angles, and it will allow you to craft a customized charm each time.

WEARABLE PROTECTION POWDER

This blend of protection powder is meant to be made into a paste that you can apply directly to your body. It is meant to repel negative energy, and it is perfect to wear when you find yourself around people who may not have your best interests at heart. Sage is cleansing, parsley promotes well-being, and rosemary clears away lingering negative energy.

WHEN TO PERFORM THE SPELL
Create this charm on a full moon or on a Sunday.

TIME TO ALLOT FOR THE SPELL
It will take about 15 minutes to gather everything you need and prepare the powder.

WHERE TO PERFORM THE SPELL
Create this in a comfortable and powerful workspace, such as your kitchen or your altar.

INGREDIENTS AND TOOLS
Splash of Florida Water
Small mason jar
2 tablespoons activated charcoal
1 tablespoon ground sage
1 tablespoon ground parsley
1 tablespoon ground rosemary
10 drops unblocking oil (similar to road opener, this is a blend that can be found in specialized shops)

1. Use the Florida Water to cleanse the mason jar. Let the jar dry completely.

2. One at a time, hold each of the rest of the ingredients in your hand. Feel the energy of each one before adding them to the mason jar. Take your time.

3. When you are ready to wear the charm, mix about a teaspoon of the jar mixture with a few drops of water to form a paste.

4. Use the paste to draw a protective sigil or symbol on your body beneath your clothing. Choose a symbol that is powerful to you or your tradition.

TIP Unblocking oil is a special oil blend that can typically be found premade in folk magic stores.

WEEKLY QUICK CLEANSING RITUAL

This is a perfect little ritual that takes less than 10 minutes. If you do it weekly, you can keep the spiritual energy in your home fresh and cleansed. It is ideal to do this after you've physically cleaned your home. Sage and salt water clears the space and the energy, while the herbs simmer on the stove, pulling in new energy to replace the cleared energy. This helps you completely refresh your space.

WHEN TO PERFORM THE SPELL
Choose a day that you regularly have available to do chores.

TIME TO ALLOT FOR THE SPELL
Give yourself about 10 minutes to prepare and complete this ritual.

WHERE TO PERFORM THE SPELL
This ritual takes place in various parts of the home.

INGREDIENTS AND TOOLS
Large pot
8 cups water
Stove top
1 piece aloe vera
1 piece orange peel
1 tablespoon dried rosemary
1 cup salt water
1 bundle sage or palo santo
1 shot rum or another libation

1. Prepare your home for cleansing by opening up your windows and making sure you have a clear path from room to room.

2. Start your simmer blend by heating a large pot of water over high heat.

3. When the water is simmering, turn the heat down to low.

4. Add the aloe vera, orange peel, and rosemary to the simmering water. Let this mixture continue to simmer until you're finished with the ritual.

5. Starting at one corner of your home, dip your fingers into the salt water and then flick water up toward where the ceiling meets the wall.

6. Start moving left, along the wall, until you have done this to all the rooms in your home.

7. Once you've finished, light your bundle of sage or palo santo so it is smoldering. Go around again, moving to the right, until every room in the home has been smudged.

8. Finally, give thanks to any spirit ancestors that protect your home by pouring them a shot of rum. Say something like "Thank you to all spirits of place, spirits in this home, and spirit guides who are watching over this home and its family. As a thank you, I give you this offering." Then pour it out onto the ground or sidewalk outside of your home.

9. Do this ritual weekly to keep the energy in your home light and cleansed, and to help prevent any negative spiritual buildup.

CAR PROTECTION CHARM

Protection while traveling is important. Keep this charm in your car's glove compartment to help protect you and your vehicle while in transit. The specific herbal blend used in this charm promotes safe travel.

WHEN TO PERFORM THE SPELL
Create this charm during a full moon.

TIME TO ALLOT FOR THE SPELL
It will take about 15 minutes to gather everything you need and assemble your charm.

WHERE TO PERFORM THE SPELL
Create this charm in a comfortable and powerful workspace, such as your kitchen or your altar.

INGREDIENTS AND TOOLS
1 tablespoon dried kelp
1 tablespoon dried feverfew
½ tablespoon dried kava kava
1 piece lucky hand root
10 drops comfrey oil
Pouch (a white one is wonderful for protection spells)

1. One at a time, hold each ingredient in your hand. Feel its individual energy.

2. Insert each item into the pouch. Take your time. Feel free to add any other symbols, herbs, or crystals not on the above list that resonate with you.

3. As you work, focus your mind on intentions of strength, protection, safety, and courage.

4. Store this charm in the glove compartment of your car, and remake it yearly based on how you feel it's working.

CLOVE PROTECTION SPELL FOR BUSY WITCHES

This spell is designed to help push away any negative influences you feel may be trying to reach you. It guards against those with poor intentions. The herbs used here not only protect against enemies but also friends who may have agendas you don't quite agree with. This spell comes to us from Austen Smith and was originally published in the September 2018 issue of *Witch Way Magazine*.

WHEN TO PERFORM THE SPELL

A full moon or a Sunday is great for this type of spell.

TIME TO ALLOT FOR THE SPELL

This spell will take about 30 minutes.

WHERE TO PERFORM THE SPELL

This spell should be done in your most spiritual space, such as your altar.

INGREDIENTS AND TOOLS

1 red, black, or white chime candle

2 tablespoons whole cloves

1 tablespoon olive oil

1 tablespoon crushed black peppercorns

1 tablespoon crushed and dried basil leaves

1 tablespoon sea salt

1. Cast your circle. Call your spirits. Ground yourself and prepare to do the work.

2. Stud the chime candle with whole cloves (i.e., press the cloves into the candle's surface) in a design of your liking.

3. Roll the candle in olive oil.

4. Lay out your black peppercorns, basil, and salt on a hard surface. Then roll the candle through this mixture.

5. Recite this affirmation (or create your own):

   I call on the Ancient Ones. The Ones who lived resolved lives and died resolved deaths. I call on those who nourish my journey toward spiritual alignment and serve as pillars in my evolution. I call on the spirit medicine of clove and accompanying herbs to unite with the Ancient Ones. Form a shield around my body, my mind, and my soul as I move forward through these difficult challenges. Let this shield protect me from harm, distraction, envy, and other destructive emotions that attempt to thwart my path. Let this spell serve as a demonstration of my faith. So it is.

6. Candle gaze (stare into the flame of the candle) to visualize your desired outcome.

7. Express gratitude for what is to come.

8. End the ritual by closing your circle.

A WITCH JAR FOR PROTECTION

Using a witch jar is a classic protection technique. In this spell, we are going to make a trap for any negative or harmful energy that is being sent your way. The sharp objects within a witch jar pull negative energy coming toward you into the jar.

WHEN TO PERFORM THE SPELL
Create this witch jar during a time you feel most magically powerful.

TIME TO ALLOT FOR THE SPELL
It will take about 30 minutes to gather everything you need and assemble your jar.

WHERE TO PERFORM THE SPELL
Create this in a comfortable and powerful workspace. If you can create it outside near a spot where it can be buried, do so.

INGREDIENTS AND TOOLS
4 cups salt
Clean glass jar with lid
Sharp objects such as glass, nails, or rusted metal, etc.
Bodily fluid that represents the witch creating the jar
Black sealing wax

1. Pour the salt into the jar.

2. Very carefully, add in your sharp objects. You want to fill the jar completely with these items.

3. Pour in your bodily fluid of choice. This will connect the jar to you.

4. Seal the jar, using black sealing wax. Make sure it is completely sealed so that it can't be opened.

5. Bury this jar on your property. If you are unable to bury the jar, keep it in a dark and quiet space where it will not be disturbed. You only have to do this once on a property. There is no need to remove buried jars. If you do remove a buried jar, throw it away.

HEX BREAKER TRIFECTA

If you believe that someone has sent some bad energy your way, this spell is perfect to help break that connection. This spell comes to us from Michelle Guerrero Denison and was originally published in the November 2016 issue of *Witch Way Magazine*.

WHEN TO PERFORM THE SPELL
A full moon or a Sunday is great for this type of spell.

TIME TO ALLOT FOR THE SPELL
This spell will take about 30 minutes.

WHERE TO PERFORM THE SPELL
This spell should be done in your most spiritual space, such as your altar or outside.

INGREDIENTS AND TOOLS
1 floating tealight candle (This is specialized to float. Other tea candles may float, but are likely to sink or get the wax wet.)
Bowl of water
1 lemon
Knife
2 cups sea salt
1 sachet
3 pieces star anise
1 teaspoon white sage
1 sprig rosemary
1 strand hair from your body
1 nail clipping from your body
1 tiger's eye gemstone

1. Float a tealight candle on the surface of the bowl of water.

2. Close your eyes and take a deep breath. Focus on stopping the misfortune and chaos that surrounds you.

3. After a few minutes, open your eyes.

4. Light the candle and set it aside.

5. Hold the lemon in your hands, and maintain your focus.

6. Repeat the phrase, "*Break this curse*," over and over until you feel the lemon has absorbed your intent.

7. Slice the lemon in half, and press it into a mound of sea salt, covering the juicy flesh with a thick layer.

8. Set the lemon aside for now.

9. Assemble your sachet. Include the star anise, white sage, rosemary, hair, nail clipping, and tiger's eye.

10. Once your candle has burnt out, dig a hole in your yard and bury the candle. Then pour the water you used over the spot.

11. Keep the sachet and the lemon on your altar until the lemon shrivels up. This may take about 2 to 3 weeks.

12. Once finished, you can bury the lemon and keep the sachet.

GLOSSARY

Below is a list of terms I've used throughout the book. For the most part, I have defined these terms in context, but I want to give you an easy place to revisit any definitions that you forget.

BOOK OF SHADOWS: This is a witch's personal record of their spell work, private thoughts, and spiritual secrets. It is sometimes coded using the Theban alphabet.

CASTING A CIRCLE: This practice creates a protected and sacred space prior to performing a ritual. Casting a circle can involve meditation, making a physical circle with crystals or candles, or even taking a protective bath.

CHIME CANDLES: Chime candles are unscented, four-inch, mini taper candles that are often used in candle magic spells. Their small size makes them easy to store and set up on an altar, and they come in many different colors.

THE CONE OF POWER: This is a method of raising energy within a magical ritual. Often the practitioner pulls the energy up from the earth and into the space they are occupying.

CROSSROADS: A crossroads is a place where two roads meet. Lost spirits often wander in and around a crossroads. For this reason, crossroads are often used as a place to leave offerings to spirits in witchcraft practices.

THE ETHER: The ether is the energetic space that fills the universe, aka the other world or the spirit world.

THE FAE: These are otherworldly creatures that come into our world through the elements. They include fairies, gnomes, dryads, trolls, changelings, and elves.

FIRE JUMPING: This is a symbolic practice that involves literally jumping over a small fire to signify the transition from our mundane world into the world of magic. It is also said to aid in warding off evil spirits in many cultures.

FLORIDA WATER: This is a cologne made from alcohol and herbs. It is typically purchased from magic shops, though Florida Water can sometimes be found in regular pharmacies in the Southern United States.

GROUNDING: This practice involves sitting within nature to calm one's mental and spiritual energy. Grounding is said to release this more chaotic energy back into the earth and away from our minds and bodies.

HERBALS: Herbs, plants, and spices used within a witchcraft practice.

LITHOMANCY: This is a form of divination that involves reading stones.

LOAS: Loas are voodoo spirits.

OOMANCY: This is a form of divination that involves reading eggs.

PYROMANCY: This is a form of divination that involves reading flames.

QUERENT: This is the term for a person seeking a tarot reading.

SABBATS: Sabbats are the eight pagan festivals celebrated by witches that correspond to the cycle of the seasons. They are Yule (around December 21), Imbolc (around February 2), Ostara (around March 20), Beltane (around May 1), Litha (around June 20), Lammas (around August 1), Mabon (around September 22), and Samhain (around November 1).

SIGILS: These are symbols that are created in order to capture and house a certain energy or intention.

SKYCLAD: This is a Wiccan term for performing rituals in the nude.

SMUDGE BUNDLE: This is a bundle of cleansing herbs like sage or palo santo wood that, when burnt, produces smoke that can clear stagnant or negative energy from a space or object. Burning a smudge bundle to clear unwanted energy is called smudging.

TRIQUETRA: A triquetra is a Celtic knot symbol that represents the power of threes, including the maiden, mother, and crone, or the past, present, and future—a never-ending cycle of life.

VEVES: This group of symbols is used within a house of Haitian voodoo to represent the astral world and different spirits.

VOID MOON: This is when the moon transits out of one sign of the zodiac and into another.

THE WHEEL OF THE YEAR: This is the modern term for the calendar of pagan celebrations.

RESOURCES

Drawing Down the Moon, **by Margot Adler**
Any good belief system needs to stem from a solid foundation. This book will not only give you a historical background on witchcraft, but it will also help you understand how it developed over the years and into so many different paths.

The Complete Book of Incense, Oils and Brews, **by Scott Cunningham**
Perfect for the herbal witch, this book has everything you need to get comfortable in the kitchen and learn new concoctions.

The Witches, Book of the Dead, **by Christian Day**
By far my favorite resource on spirts and spirit work, this book is the best guide I've found that can help any witch who feels connected to the spirit world.

A Curious Future, **by Kiki Dombrowski**
This book is a comprehensive guide for those new to divination. You get thorough explanations of all kinds of divination techniques, and it gives you enough information to research more on your own.

Eight Extraordinary Days, **by Kiki Dombrowski**
The Wheel of the Year plays a large part in how many witches
practice. This book goes through each season, as well as covers
recipes and exercises you can do to connect to the energy of the
earth as it turns throughout the year.

The Art of Witch, **by Fiona Horne**
What does it mean to be a witch? This book answers that question and more. A rulebook for the rebels, it talks about how your
life changes as a witch.

The Encyclopedia of Occultism and Parapsychology, **edited by
J. Gordon Melton**
This is an amazing resource for any witch. Look up practices,
names, spirits, and terms. The best part is that this encyclopedia
will give you a scientific explanation while also giving you stud-
ies to look into further.

Witch Way Magazine
A modern lifestyle magazine on witchcraft (mine!). Ignite new
passions or gain new perspectives on your favorite old traditions.

Get Psychic! **by Stacey Wolf**
This is a wonderfully fun book that will help you pinpoint your
psychic gifts and learn exercises to develop them. It does so in a
fun and engaging way that is easy enough for a witch of any level.
It's full of quizzes, stories, and exercises. *Get Psychic!* is a great
book to read right after *The Door to Witchcraft.*

REFERENCES

Adler, Margot. *Drawing Down the Moon: Witches, Druids, Goddess-Worshippers, and Other Pagans in America Today.* New York: Penguin Books, 1997.

Ben-Yehuda, Nachman. "The European Witch Craze of the 14th to 17th Centuries: A Sociologist's Perspective." *American Journal of Sociology* 86, no. 1 (July 1980): 1–31. https://doi.org/10.1086/227200.

Brown, Tonya. "Charge an Item with Spirit Protection." *Witch Way Magazine*, August 1, 2016.

—. "Passion Candles." *Witch Way Magazine*, February 1, 2017.

—. "Pizza to Mend Strained Relationships." *Witch Way Magazine*, September 1, 2018.

—. "Reading Tea Leaves." *Witch Way Magazine*, November 2015.

Denison, Michelle Guerreo. "Hex Breaker Trifecta." *Witch Way Magazine*, November 2016.

Dombrowski, Kiki. *A Curious Future: A Handbook of Unusual Divination and Unique Oracular Techniques.* Nashville: Phoebe Publishing, 2018.

—. *Eight Extraordinary Days: Celebrations, Mythology, Magic, and Divination for the Witches' Wheel of the Year.* Nashville: Phoebe Publishing, 2017.

—. "In the Classroom: Exploring Elemental Magic with Fiona Horne." *Witch Way Magazine*, July 1, 2018

—. "Kiki's Oil Grimoire." *Witch Way Magazine*, March 2018.

—. "Modern Day Flying Witches Ointment." *Witch Way Magazine*, November 1, 2016.

Donsbach, Margaret. "Boudica: Celtic War Queen Who Challenged Rome." *HistoryNet*, June 12, 2006. http://www.historynet.com /boudica-celtic-war-queen-who-challenged-rome.htm.

Duplass, Mark and Jay Duplass, dir. *Jeff, Who Lives at Home*. Hollywood, CA: Paramount Vantage, 2012.

English Oxford Living Dictionaries, s.v. "pagan," accessed January 21, 2019. https://en.oxforddictionaries.com/definition/pagan.

Fleming, Andrew, dir. *The Craft*. Culver City, CA: Columbia Pictures, 1996.

Garber, Megan. "Why Do Witches Ride Brooms? (NSFW)." *The Atlantic*, October 31, 2013. https://www.theatlantic.com/technology /archive/2013/10/why-do-witches-ride-brooms-nsfw/281037/.

Grohol, John M. "15 Common Cognitive Distortions." *PsychCentral*, accessed October 28, 2018. https://psychcentral.com/lib /15-common-cognitive-distortions/.

Herkes, Michael. "Interview with Austin Shippey." *Witch Way Magazine*, January 2018.

—. "Lustcraft." *Witch Way Magazine*, February 1, 2018.

Horne, Fiona. *7 Days to Magickal New You*. London: Thorsons, 2001.

—. *The Naked Witch: An Autobiography*. Dulwich Hill, AU: Rockpool Publishing, 2018.

—. *Witch: A Magickal Journey*. London: Thorsons, 2002.

The International Center for Reiki Training. "Reiki." Accessed October 28, 2018. http://reiki.org.

Jacobson, Abbi, dir. *Broad City*. Season 4, episode 6, "Witches." Aired October 25, 2017, on Comedy Central.

Lester, Meera. *The Secret Power of You: Decode Your Hidden Destiny with Astrology, Tarot, Palmistry, Numerology, and the Enneagram.* Avon, MA: Adams Media, 2012.

Miiller, Em. "Tonic for Good Health." *Witch Way Magazine,* July 1, 2018.

Penczak, Christopher. *The Inner Temple of Witchcraft: Magick, Meditation and Psychic Development.* Woodbury, MN: Llewellyn Publications, 2012.

Poehler, Amy. *Yes Please.* New York: Dey Street Books, 2015.

Renton, Daina and Tonya Brown. "Red Flags When Looking for a Coven." *Witch Way Magazine,* April 2016.

Smith, Austen. "Clove Protection Spell for the Busy Witch." *Witch Way Magazine,* September 1, 2018.

Thurston, Robert. *The Witch Hunts: A History of the Witch Persecutions in Europe and North America.* Abingdon-on-Thames, UK: Routledge, 2006.

Waldman, Katy. "Why Do Witches Wear Pointy Hats?" *Slate,* October 17, 2013. http://www.slate.com/blogs/the_eye/2013/10/17/the_history_of_the_witch_s_hat_origins_of_its_pointy_design.html.

Wigington, Patti. "Warning Signs in Prospective Covens." *ThoughtCo.,* last modified June 26, 2017. https://www.thoughtco.com/warning-signs-in-prospective-covens-2562848.

Wolf, Stacey. *Get Psychic! Discover Your Hidden Powers.* New York: Grand Central Publishing, 2001.

INDEX

A

Abundance mindset, 31–32
Adler, Margot, 14, 19, 20, 77
Air, 25
Alchemy, 79
Alexandrian Wicca, 10, 22, 60, 74
Altars, 70–71
Athames, 75

B

Bells, 75
Beltane, 64–65
Black cats, 29
Black hats, 30
Book of shadows, 81
Brooms, 29, 75
Burning Times, 18

C

Calendars and cycles, 61
Candles, 49, 76
Card readings, 45–46
Career spells
    Charm for Finding a
      Job, 124–125
    Fast Money-Drawing
      Oil, 130–131
    Honey Jar for Sweet
      Words, 128–129
    intention-setting, 123
    Power-of-Three Interview
      Oil, 134–135
    Ritual to Attain Long-Term
      Goals, 132–133
    Success-in-Business
      Oil, 126–127

Cauldrons, 76
Ceremonies, 60
Chalices, 76
Change, creating, 36–37
Chants, 68
Charms, 49, 165
Christianity, 16–17, 29
Circles, 57, 79
"Clair"-abilities, 51–53
Clothing, 73–74
Colors, 84–85
Cone of power, 30
Cooking magic, 137, 141
Correspondences, 30–31
Cosmos, 27–28
Covens, 5, 56–60
Crystals, 49, 76

D

Days of the week, 61–62
Déjà vu, 54
Devil worship, 29
Dianic Wicca, 22
Divination, 36, 50
Dombrowski, Kiki, 41, 46, 134, 154
Dreams, 55
Dyer, Mary, 19

E

Earth, 24, 26
Eclectic witches, 10
Elements, 24–25
Energy, 7, 8, 23–25, 27–30,
    49–50
Environment, 23–25

F

Feminine energy, 7
Feri Tradition, 22
Fertility, 25–28
Fire, 25
Florida water, 49–50
Folk witches, 9–10
Free will, 36
Friends and family matters spells
    Candle Spell to Help a
        Friend During Emotional
        Hardship, 138–139
    Freezer Spell to Remove a
        Toxic Person from Your
        Life, 148–149
    Friendship-Healing Spell
        Candles, 142–143
    Herkimer-Diamond
        Talisman, 146–147
    intention-setting, 137
    Pizza to Mend Strained
        Friendships, 140–141
    Witch Ball for Family
        Abundance, 144–145

G

Gardner, Gerald, 19
Gardnerian Wicca, 10, 21–22
Glam witches, 9
Gods and goddesses, 80–81
Good vs. evil, ideas of, 33–34
Gratitude, 31–32
Green witches, 9

H

Health and healing spells
    Charm to Promote Physical
        Healing, 114–115
    General Spell for Well-Being and
        Abundance, 116–117
    intention-setting, 109
    Moon-Glow Oil, 120–121
    Pain-Release Ritual, 118–119
    Promote Health in a Sick
        Household, 110–111
    Tonic for Good Health, 112–113
Helping others, 32–33

Herbs, 49, 77, 109
Hymns, 68

I

Imbolc, 63–64
Incense, 77
Innocent VIII, pope, 19
Intention, 36
Intuition, 28–30, 50–55

K

Karma, 35
Knots, 79
Kramer, Heinrich, 13, 18, 19
Kyteler, Alice, 12, 17, 19

L

Lammas, 65–66
Lenormand cards, 45
Litha, 65
Lotions, 151
Love spells
    Attention-Drawing Lustcraft
        Oil, 104–105
    Breakup Forward Movement
        Spell, 102–103
    Candle Ritual to Draw Love
        Near, 100–101
    Charm for Confidence and
        Self-Love, 94–95
    intention-setting, 91
    Love-Drawing Oil, 98–99
    Quick Passion Candles, 92–93
    Ritual for Honoring Yourself as a
        God/Goddess, 106–107
    Sugar Jar for Sweet
        Thoughts, 96–97
Lunar energy, 7

M

Mabon, 66
Magic, 69–70, 137, 141. *See
    also* Spells
*Malleus Maleficarum (Hammer
    of Witches)*, 13, 18
Masculine energy, 7

Meditation, 38
Moon, 27–28, 67–68, 106
Murray, Margaret, 19

N

Names, 81
Nature, 23–25
Necromancers, 10

O

Oils, 77, 99, 109, 123, 167
Oracle cards, 45
Ostara, 64
Ouija boards, 48

P

Paganism, 4, 14–16
Palm readings, 42–44
Pendulums, 48
Pentacles, 78
Pentagrams, 78
Premonitions, 55
Protection spells
    Car Protection Charm, 170–171
    Clove Protection Spell for Busy
        Witches, 172–173
    Hex Breaker Trifecta, 176–177
    intention-setting, 165
    Wearable Protection
        Powder, 166–167
    Weekly Quick Cleansing
        Ritual, 168–169
    A Witch Jar for
        Protection, 174–175
Psychic abilities, 50–55

R

Reiki, 38
Rituals, 60, 71–72
Runes, 46

S

Sabbats, 62–67
Salem witch trials, 18

Samhain, 67
Scrying, 41–42
Seasons, 62
Sexuality, 25–28
Sigils, 79
Silence, vows of, 40
Solar energy, 7
Songs, 68–69
Sorcerers, 10
Spells, 58, 72–73, 88–89, 91. See
    also specific
Spirit (element), 25
Spirit realm, 28
Spiritual work spells
    Building a Spirit Altar, 152–153
    Classic Dreamer's Tea, 156–157
    Divination Oil, 160–161
    intention-setting, 151
    Kiki's Flying Witches
        Ointment, 154–155
    Petition a Spirit for
        Assistance, 158–159
    Spell to Charge an Item with
        Spirit Protection, 162–163
Statues, 77
Symbols, 78–80

T

Tarot cards, 45, 46
Tasseography, 47
Tea leaf reading, 47
Theban alphabet, 81–83
Tools, 75–78
Totems, 79
Traditional witches, 10, 60
Triangles, 78–79

V

Veves, 80
Visioning, 39

W

Wands, 75
Warlocks, 10
Water, 25
Wheel of the Year, 14–15

White light, 49
Wicca, 4, 20–22
Willpower, 39
Witchcraft
   defined, 2–4
   history of, 11–21
   and womanhood, 7

Witches
   defined, 3–4
   inclinations of, 6–9
   misconceptions about, 5–6
   origins of rumors about, 29–30
   types of, 9–10

Y

Yule, 63

ACKNOWLEDGMENTS

I'd like to thank all of the people who helped me write this book: Fiona Horne for being a selfless giver of spiritual guidance, Paul Flagg for just dealing with me in general, Michael Herkes for helping carry my *Witch Way* workload when I was writing this book, Kiki Dombrowski for being the purest soul I will ever meet, and Houngan Matt for being always ready with advice. I'd also like to thank all of my *Witch Way* family, including Michelle Guerrero Denison, Em Miiller, and Austen Smith, for being with me on this crazy wonderful journey.

ABOUT THE AUTHOR

TONYA A. BROWN is a current resident of New Orleans, Louisiana, where she is the editor-in-chief of *Witch Way Magazine* and runs a small apothecary out of her home. Prior to her time in New Orleans, Tonya lived in Tampa, Florida, where she received her bachelor's degree in psychology from the University of Tampa and her associate's degree in computer analysis. Tonya began writing for *Witch Way Magazine* and dedicated her life to supporting the creative pursuits of other witches. While this is the first book she's authored, this is not the first magical book she's consulted on.

Tonya is active in the spiritual community of New Orleans, where she prefers to remain a helpful support system behind the scenes. Tonya is a Lenormand reader, medium, and magical guide for other witches. Having extensively studied divination, parapsychology, and the occult, Tonya has been a teacher at pagan and witchcraft events across the South. Tonya can be found at www.SimplyIrresistibleMagic.com.

Printed in the USA
CPSIA information can be obtained
at www.ICGtesting.com
CBHW041134270224
4709CB00005B/18